The
Business *of*
Portfolio Management

Boosting Organizational Value Through
Portfolio Management

Iain Fraser
Dip PPC, PMP, MoP, P3M3, PMI Fellow, Fellow PMINZ

Library of Congress Cataloging-in-Publication Data

Names: Fraser, Iain, 1955- author.
Title: The business of portfolio management / Iain Fraser.
Description: Newtown Square : Project Management Institute, 2017. | Includes
  bibliographical references and index.
Identifiers: LCCN 2017015585 (print) | LCCN 2017021942 (ebook) | ISBN 9781628253733 (ePub) |
  ISBN 9781628253740 (Kindle) | ISBN 9781628253757 (Web PDF) | ISBN
  9781628253726 (hardback)
Subjects: LCSH: Project management. | Organizational change. | Leadership. |
  BISAC: BUSINESS & ECONOMICS / Project Management.
Classification: LCC HD69.P75 (ebook) | LCC HD69.P75 F7377 2017 (print) | DDC 658.4--dc23
LC record available at https://lccn.loc.gov/2017015585

ISBN: 978-1-62825-372-6

Published by: Project Management Institute, Inc.
            14 Campus Boulevard
            Newtown Square, Pennsylvania 19073-3299 USA
            Phone: +610-356-4600
            Fax: +610-356-4647
            Email: customercare@pmi.org
            Internet: PMI.org

PMI Publications welcomes corrections and comments on its books. Please feel free to send
comments on typographical, formatting, or other errors. Simply make a copy of the relevant
page of the book, mark the error, and send it to: Book Editor, PMI Publications, 14 Campus
Boulevard, Newtown Square, PA 19073-3299 USA.

To inquire about discounts for resale or educational purposes, please contact the PMI Book
Service Center.

            PMI Book Service Center
            P.O. Box 932683, Atlanta, GA 31193-2683 USA
            Phone: 1-866-276-4764 (within the U.S. or Canada) or +1-770-280-4129 (globally)
            Fax: +1-770-280-4113
            Email: info@bookorders.pmi.org

Contents

Dedication

To my darling wife,
Britta, and to my two fabulous sons,
Ollie and Pat. You inspired and supported me
to get this finished. I thank each of you
immensely for encouraging
me to keep going.

Also to my late father,
John (Ian) L. Fraser who, somewhat unwittingly,
inspired in me a lifelong desire to do
better in all aspects of life.

Acknowledgments

First, and generally, to the countless people from around the world whom I have met during my career and have had the pleasure to spend time with, I thank each of you. You have all contributed in some way to my career learning and to my thoughts, many of which are reflected in this work.

Special thanks go to the following:

The Project Management Institute (PMI) for agreeing to publish the book and for the support from various individuals within PMI, and also for permission to use various diagrams from their excellent standards and original research titles.

Change Consultants LLC for permission to refer to their change management model.

Human Systems International for permission to refer to the Quadrant (4Q) Assessment model.

Project Plus Ltd. for permission to mention the 4-P Methodology™ and Compass Assessment™ frameworks.

The Government of Samoa for permission to use *The Switch* steps associated with the September 2009 driving change. Thanks also to Belinda Filo-Tafunai of the Samoa High Commission in Wellington for her support.

Van Morrill of Harvard Business Publishing for permission to use Daniel Goleman's *Leadership That Gets Results* extract.

To the publishers of the books referenced in the text that graciously allowed me to use some of their respective material from the sources listed in the Glossary.

To David Pells, who unselfishly and graciously provided the Foreword. Those words create such a relevant and insightful stage for the content that follows. Thank you again, David!

To the group of reviewers who willingly and generously gave their time and intellect to review the book prior to publishing. Thank you to Craig Bunyan, Louis Mercken, Rommy Musch, Sarah Ross, Mark Sanborn, and Chris Till.

To Gabrielle Parle, who provided valuable feedback following the professional proofread she conducted on the completed manuscript.

I acknowledge all who were mentioned above and all the other wonderful support I received with deep gratitude and humility.

About the Author

Iain Fraser
Dip PPC, PMP, MoP, P3M3, PMI
Fellow, Fellow PMINZ
E: iain.fraser@jacobite.co.nz
T: +64 21 479 301
LinkedIn: www.linkedin.com/
pub/iain-fraser/0/2b1/8a4

A proud Scot from the Highlands of Scotland, now living in New Zealand and working around the world, Iain is globally recognized for his expertise, experience, and insights on portfolio, program, and project management approaches. He consults, writes, speaks, and trains through his company, Jacobite Consulting Ltd. Iain is a member of the *globalScot* business network and also sits on a number of "for-profit" and advisory boards and is a chartered member of the Institute of Directors.

Iain is considered a thought leader by his peers. He has been featured on live radio, TV, video, and podcasts, and is often quoted in print media, including *The Times* and *The Telegraph* of the United Kingdom.

He is founder and former CEO of Project Plus Ltd., a management consulting organization that focuses on the provision of project-based and business management services across industry sectors and delivered globally. Iain is a past chair of the PMI Board of Directors and served six years on the global board, overseeing a period of considerable growth and global expansion.

In 2009, he was awarded PMI Fellow status in recognition of his significant contributions to the global portfolio, program, and project management profession.

Foreword

Portfolio management is one of the most important developments in business management of the past few decades. As more organizations and entire industries around the world have become more project-based, the importance of aligning programs and projects with business strategies has become more and more critical. Beyond strategic alignment, though, good portfolio management goes straight to the heart of organizational strategy itself, the creation of value.

Effective portfolio management allows organizations and executives to ensure that all major investments in programs and projects support strategic objectives so that successful program and project management then supports the achievement of those business goals. The portfolio management process reinforces the need for effective and efficient project management at the operational level. More important, effective portfolio management includes a disciplined process for identifying, prioritizing, and selecting the right programs and projects as well as other work. If the wrong projects are selected and initiated, effective program or project management will be for naught. Only the selection and successful implementation of the right projects can result in the maximum creation of business value.

Value creation in projects has another dimension that is too often overlooked. That is the opposite result when programs and projects fail—value destruction. The continuing poor track record for program and project management in some industries is well known, for example, the high failure rate of large IT projects or those with too much complexity. A failed project can lead to financial losses, lost customers, tarnished reputations, broken careers, and even business failure. This is another reason why portfolio management is now so critical. The right project done wrong or the wrong project being done at all—these can lead to value destruction. The right project done right leads to value creation!

That is why this new book by Iain Fraser is so timely and important. His value management framework is brilliant. There is no question that it will help executives, business managers, portfolio managers, and even program/project managers focus on the important steps to maximizing value. This is a big deal! It can help businesses become more innovative, more profitable, more sustainable, and more successful in today's very competitive global economy.

Effective portfolio management requires successful organizational change, however; this is not always easy. This is especially true for organizations that have historically been organized and managed as ongoing operations, with functional departments aligned with manufacturing processes, products, markets, or geography. A growing percentage of an organization's business (and the global economy) is through programs and projects; however, organizations must change. They must ensure that the right projects are selected, implemented, and support business strategy—their projects must create value. Organizational change must lead to more value creation.

Implementing portfolio management through effective organizational change management is the focus of Sections 3 and 4 of this book. Program management is also explained in the context of realizing benefits and creating value. These are critical aspects of introducing portfolio management to any organization, be it a for-profit, nonprofit, or governmental enterprise.

The project, program, and portfolio management fields are maturing rapidly. There are now many good books about these topics, and thousands of articles and papers. I've had occasion to publish many in our *PM World Journal*. I know many of the authors and experts advancing professional practice in these fields. But this is not a book about project or program management. It's an executive guide to implementing effective portfolio management.

I have known Iain Fraser for more than 20 years and am fully aware of his contributions to the project management profession, including his leadership in New Zealand and his service on the global Project Management Institute's (PMI) Board of Directors (including serving as chair of the Board). I am familiar with some of his projects and management consulting activities throughout the regions of Asia-Pacific, Europe, and North America. We have had numerous occasions over the years to meet and discuss projects, business, and management topics. I was therefore happy to learn about his new book, hoping that he would share some of the knowledge he has gained over his 30+ year career. I am now even happier to have had a chance to read this fine new book, *The Business of Portfolio Management*.

What's even better, it's a short, simple executive guide, easily readable in a couple of hours. This is a good book! It will be very helpful to executives and managers of all organizations with projects—those who want to implement portfolio management in order to help their organizations maximize value and be more successful.

David L. Pells
PMI Fellow, HonFellow APM (UK)
Managing Editor, *PM World Journal*
Addison, Texas, USA

Introduction

I have always enjoyed writing. I have jotted down many of my ideas and shared them in white papers, training materials, and booklets for many years. Many of these materials have been published around the world in various business magazines, social media, radio, and media outlets.

I have, for some time, had the desire to write a business management book on the impact that the project management profession, and portfolio management in particular, can have on the development and implementation of strategy and for better organizational performance.

I remain inspired by the visions and guidance offered by Tom Peters and Robert Waterman, and Jim Collins in their respective megasellers, *In Search of Excellence: Changing the Way the World Does Business* and *Good to Great: Why Some Companies Make the Leap and Others Don't*. These books have surely guided countless leaders and managers around the world to better things for the past few decades. Perhaps, though, there is an additional and more modern need that builds on these giant works, and it is my wish that this book will be the next milestone of organizational performance guidance.

I wanted the content to reflect my 30-year business experience gained in a variety of sectors as well as my vision and collated thoughts on strategic implementation. I intend for this book to be hard-hitting in some aspects, but also a pragmatic guide that readers can leverage to reset their organizations using the power of value-driven portfolio management as the bridge that links strategy and its implementation.

During the early phases of writing, I became concerned that my suggested implementation of portfolio management would be interpreted by many as a recommendation for another set of mid-level processes. Not so! Those, if added to existing processes would, I thought, further hamper the organization from being nimble, adaptable to change, and efficient. To that end, I have devised a value management framework that I believe can act as a tool for strategic planning and its implementation management. It can also maintain alignment of strategic desire with day-to-day implementation activities. This book explains what the value management framework is and how it can be applied to all aspects of strategy implementation management.

I have tried to align or adapt much of the content to the global standards and other publications issued by the Project Management Institute (PMI). This is to provide a level of commonality and consistency to readers irrespective of their location. I have used American English in favor of other versions, as the book is to be published in the United States for a global audience.

I have included a number of selected case studies to demonstrate or emphasize certain points. These, in most cases, are based on actual experiences I have had the good fortune to be involved with. The book is written in four sections, so that readers can quickly find references and guidance to specific components they seek.

Section 1 sets the tone and suggests why a radical transformation is required in most workplaces. This proposition is based on the need to be better, to adapt, and to capitalize on new opportunities. It is also based on the need to exploit the underutilized mechanism that is portfolio management. The introduction of a value management framework allows for the development and alignment of strategy that is more realistic, less abstract, and thereby has a higher probability of being implemented successfully.

Section 2 discusses and details portfolio management, or "a way of doing business," as I have defined it. This mechanism is pitched at a higher level than the commonly talked about project portfolio management. Portfolio management in this manner allows for operational expenditure (opex) and strategic capital expenditure (capex) to be planned in unison to allow for a more balanced portfolio(s) and for more value to be captured. These portfolios would replace today's typical short-term business plans.

Section 3 lays out implementation and delivery techniques, termed *programs of work,* which is my term for blending opex and capex activity into plans for more efficient implementation. For completeness, it also provides a short commentary on project management as a delivery vehicle within programs of work.

Section 4 highlights the leadership aspects that are required to implement the many suggestions the book offers. It also presents a compelling change management discussion. Required change associated with future contributions from corporate support functions is also discussed. Some specific guidance is offered on roles, responsibilities, and professional development for key portfolio and program of work staff.

Finding time was always a challenge, so the encouragement from family and friends has been fantastic and hugely motivational. This book is the result, and I hope that you enjoy reading it. It is my intention that you will gain knowledge you can use to transform your organization and improve its activity and performance. By doing that, your organization will become a consistently high-performing entity that others will aspire toward.

Thank you for buying this book. Do please get in touch should you wish to.

Slainte Mhath! (To your good health!)

Continuous effort—not strength or intelligence—
is the key to unlocking our potential.

—Winston Churchill

Organizational Woes and Wishes

1-1. Staying in Business Versus Getting Ahead

The global financial crisis (GFC) of late 2008 made us all very aware of the damage to businesses and economies that a few reckless, overly optimistic, and—according to many—very irresponsible people can cause. Even today, economies are still struggling to recover while many businesses have simply disappeared, leaving a degree of carnage behind. There is still some debate on just how successful initiatives from the era of government stimulus were in terms of improving local economic well-being.

According to the Economist Intelligence Unit, the next decade is likely to see global growth of just 3.5% per year. This suggests fewer opportunities for the majority of businesses unless they adopt some new form—unless they innovate and change. Indeed, the post-GFC has forced many organizational leaders to focus on the need for change to combat new market mantras and fierce, and in many cases, global competition. I refer to the market mantras as "better, faster, cheaper" in the for-profit sectors and "doing more for less" in the nonprofit sectors. Those mantras are driving leaders to seek better ways of achieving their respective organizational goals and objectives. Initially, it seems that the need to speed up, to increase effectiveness, and to remain nimble are the top challenges. Further thought, however, suggests that talent management, that is, developing people and culture at *all* levels of an organization, is the catalyst for the sustainable organizational change required to respond to these mantras.

It seems that there is a "reset" opportunity here where we establish new models and systems that will guide us to create highly nimble organizations that are lean and fast, yet strategically focused. However, never before have organizational leaders at all levels been so challenged in their quest to adapt to the new reality of the post-GFC world. This need to adapt is being undermined by the legacy of the very same organizational structures and their leaders' inability to change quickly and adopt new business models. I refer to the ongoing, mind-numbing practice of organizational reforms that focus only on cost cutting through talent reduction. There seems to be a reluctance to move from traditional, functional structure models to the adoption of matrix management models that empower people to become more market driven, and thereby, their organizations to be more responsive enterprises.

So what to do? Stay in the same business model and risk or deny the reach of change? Or look forward and lead and change for the future by adopting new ways of working? There certainly are risks either way and perhaps a degree of comfort in the first option. However, it is the second option that will steer us toward future success and the change in culture that is the foundation for sustaining success.

1-2. Driving Value and Becoming Aligned

Today, it seems that many organizations have a gap between what is planned at a strategic level and what is actually done at a tactical or operational level. Indeed, I believe that the term *strategy* is overused, possibly abused, by many middle and senior managers who spend time producing what really is an operational plan that is labeled "strategic," typically, it seems, because it spans more than one year of operational activity. Bizarre, for sure!

To ensure organizational benefits, a primary driver for all investment decisions must be better alignment to the overarching organizational strategy through goals and objectives and short to midterm plans (say two to five years). This would contribute more value toward those goals and objectives, and ultimately, the strategy as a whole. Business leaders should already know that there are two major groups of investment within an organization, that is, those that are derived from operational activity, or "business as usual" (BAU), which typically protects existing value, and those that are derived from new strategy and the desire to change in order to gain new benefits and new value.

Figure 1-1 outlines the correlation between the value drivers and investment initiatives. I refer to it as "the continuum of investment" model.

The continuum of investment model presents the two major types of investment activity within any organization

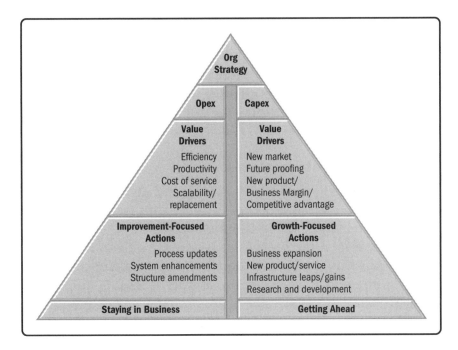

Figure 1-1: The continuum of investment.

(i.e., operational expenditure and strategic capital expenditure), often referred to as "opex" and "capex." Both of these should be delivered by planned programs of work and projects that collectively achieve or contribute to the achievement of the organizational strategy's business objectives. These collections are referred to as portfolios. The continuum of investment model can greatly help determine how proposed investments are categorized and grouped into their respective portfolios and related programs of work.

A number of factors will influence the types of projects deployed within an organization. A shift toward a market-driven operational strategy that is implemented using portfolio management will allow the organization to gain more benefits, as the portfolios will be aligned with business priorities. Corresponding programs of work and projects are better influenced as a consequence.

A considerable benefit from a market-driven approach is that of an aligned set of variables that focus on optimizing the strategic and the tangible, usually financial, value of each portfolio. This focus revolves around the following critical elements:

- Identifying and assessing the content of each portfolio;
- Weighing, prioritizing, and balancing the content of each portfolio against all work; and
- Monitoring and analyzing the value, risks, and expected results of each portfolio.

Value Management Framework

Those critical elements lead us to a value management framework to assist in establishing a strategy that focuses on organizational objectives and that can be communicated, executed, and confirmed throughout the entire organization. A value management framework encompasses the overall strategic framework for optimizing investment, its function, and its return. It utilizes five elements: value strategy, value planning, value engineering, value delivery, and value capture. As you can attest, this value management framework expands the classic element of value engineering considerably and provides a comprehensive mechanism for the wholesale determining of strategy as well as for the implementation of that strategy via the adoption of portfolio management across the organization. Without a value management framework, the deployment of portfolio management would likely tend to adopt a process-driven mentality, as opposed to the culture-driven mentality that the value management framework offers.

This new form of developing business plans from strategy needs to display certain aspects that confirm the alignment with a market-driven approach. Some examples include a strategic approach to planning versus a tactical approach; a goal-oriented vision, as opposed to a cost-oriented one; and a "time to value" culture versus a "get the job done" project execution attitude.

However, a caution should be noted at this point, as a market-driven approach to operational strategy can be hampered, and often is, by the following factors:

- Board members', executives', and senior managers' reluctance to change quickly;
- Organizational portfolio, program, and project management maturity and capability;
- Cost reduction versus investment opportunities;
- Alignment of value drivers versus available resources (budget, people, capacity, etc.); and
- Risk versus reward and unexpected compliance requirements.

These challenges can be overcome with strong leadership that uses knowledge-based decision making as a philosophy for aligning what needs to be done and what should be done. Four questions can be adopted to guide and inform the dialogue around important decisions that are required to strike the balance between "staying in business" and "getting ahead." The questions are as follows:

1. What do we know about our strategic position in regard to the capacity and capability of our organization that is relevant to this decision?

2. What do we know about our customer/client needs, wants, and preferences that is relevant to this decision?
3. What do we know about the current and evolving dynamics in the marketplace or sectors that is relevant to this decision?
4. What are the ethical and environmental implications of our choices?

The above, when considered from a value management perspective, can foster a wider and deeper understanding of each investment decision, associated time to benefits, and corresponding value capture. The questions should also assist in identifying mega-issues, or strategic risks that governance groups can further consider as necessary.

The greater the demand for investment in operations, the greater the likelihood of short-term, output-focused projects that may not deliver expected value toward business objectives. Conversely, new strategy investment projects often have a longer-term focus. There are obvious variations to this depending on the needs of the organization. However, there is a risk that with too much short-term focus, the organization will drift away from its strategy. The solution is to use the value management framework to anchor the agreed-upon goals and objectives of the organization's strategic plan to the content of each portfolio. This will greatly assist in achieving balance across both opex and capex investments.

What Is Value Management?

It is important to clarify the meaning of value management; it is not the same as value engineering. Value management focuses on organizational objectives, whereas value engineering typically focuses on the objectives of approved initiatives (e.g., project outputs). Value management encompasses the overall and strategic process of optimizing investment, its function, and its return. It utilizes the five phases referred to earlier (i.e., value strategy, value planning, value engineering, value delivery, and value capture) to achieve those.

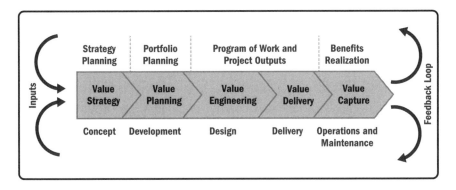

Figure 1-2:   Value management life cycle.

Value management delivers most benefits in response to a functional specification, because there is much more flexibility for optimization and for change. It is more difficult to apply value management to specific or detailed specifications/user requirements because of constraints around the specifics.

Figure 1-2 shows a value management life cycle based on the model discussed above.

Value Management and Portfolio Management

To fully optimize business benefits, an organization seeking to use the value management framework must have a solid strategy around its deployment. This strategy should include the existence of some level of portfolio management that supports option taking and decision making. Value management should provide the framework that devises a better strategy and a management approach to its implementation that ensures that the maximum value is captured and gained from each investment.

However, this alone may not provide clear benefits if it is not embedded with other key strategic approaches. A mature view of portfolio management should include the use of a value management framework as one of its key methods. When these two key approaches are combined, significant gains should be available to the organization. Table 1-1 reflects a model of integrating

Table 1-1: Value management model in a portfolio management environment.

Value Management Component	Organizational Project Management Component	Comment
Value Strategy	Strat planning and budget planning Overall implementation management	Policy to guide strategic alignment and adoption.
Value Planning	Portfolio management	Includes option analysis, selection, and prioritization.
Value Engineering	Program and project management	Develops chosen solution further. Improves inherent value. Enhances opportunities.
Value Delivery	Program and project management	Controls change and risk Protects value.
Value Capture	Benefits realization	Confirms value achieved over defined time periods. Optimizes whole of life cost versus return on investment.

value management with portfolio management. (Note that portfolio management is referred to, by some, as organizational project management.)

The value management framework, when integrated with portfolio management, provides a mechanism for key decisions to be made from rational, objective, and accountable methods. These decisions aim to achieve optimal value from the delivered functions at the least cost while meeting quality and other objectives. Value is then protected or enhanced by the structured application of value planning, value engineering, value delivery, and value capture. These phases are defined and explained in the following sections.

Value Planning

Value planning is the approach used to plan the introduction of value (e.g., saving time, increasing profit, improving quality, expanding market share, or solving problems) and to optimize organizational benefits and protect them from life cycle costs. Value planning should allow for periodic assessments/reviews so that value planned is protected and confirmed during the value delivery period. Value planning activities must be managed well and possibly throughout the entire value management cycle, but with an emphasis on the front end of a portfolio, program of work, or project. Typically, a consultative or collaborative approach would be adopted with critiques being done via value workshops. Various options would be considered in a value planning workshop and agreed-upon criteria compared against one another to allow selection decisions to be made in much the same way as portfolio planning is done. Those decisions would then provide key inputs into respective business cases or work authorization control mechanisms.

Outputs from the value planning stage would also include content for use in validating budgets and life cycle time periods as well as a value-for-money report. A value-for-money report should present the key findings and decisions made and a schedule that shows the overall life cycle of the proposed investment. A value-for-money report would typically comment on the following key sections:

1. Achieving Objectives: showing how the proposed investment will deliver benefits toward one or more objectives of the business plan, portfolio, or program of work;
2. Governance: suggesting the governance structure, methods, and key approvals that are required;
3. Critical Success Factors: highlighting the critical success factors from the proposed investment;
4. Achieving the Right Price: showing how the optimized scope delivers value-for-money in terms of capital and maintenance costs or whole-of-life costs;
5. Investment Risks: highlighting how the organization or delivery team intends to manage or improve the risk profile for the proposed initiative;
6. Non-Cost Performance: showing how non-cost performance aspects will be delivered and controlled;
7. Compliance: confirming legal and other compliance requirements; and
8. Alternatives: commenting on alternatives that were considered, assessed, and ranked/discounted.

It is the value-for-money report that bridges the void between the desired strategy of the organization and the portfolio(s) of work that are to be done to achieve the strategy—or, put another way, the improved determination of strategy. The value-for-money report can also provide quality inputs toward business cases.

Value Engineering

Value engineering provides a framework to ensure that necessary functions are achieved for optimal cost without detriment to the quality, performance, maintenance, or delivery of the defined outputs. Value engineering is typically done once the value-for-money report is available, and should focus on further developing the selected option and targeted outputs further within the business case constraints. The objective is to maximize the value and financial return against the investment cost. It includes value-for-money optimization.

The above fits nicely with the United Kingdom–based Association of Project Management's view that "value engineering is concerned with optimising the conceptual, technical and operational aspects of a project's deliverables" (APM, Section 2.3).

The ultimate objective of any value engineering activity is to identify and consider possible approaches, analyze them, and select a solution that delivers the best value to the organization and others while keeping the overall business case parameters and specifically the benefits to be gained intact. Note, though, that the best value for money does not necessarily mean the lowest cost of either capex or opex investments.

Value engineering is often done via a series of workshops similar to those done in the value planning stage. Value engineering workshops should aim to seek out as many alternatives as possible, analyze them, and select a preferred option using agreed-upon criteria that satisfy the planned output required. Risk and opportunity management would normally be done in parallel with this. Value engineering is normally quite specific in its focus and therefore tends to consider effects on cost, time, risk, and quality associated with producing the output plus operation and other life cycle costs for a whole-of-life view. Including representatives from your supply chain in value engineering workshops makes good sense, especially if members of the supply chain provide specialized products or services that are to be incorporated into the chosen solution.

These value engineering workshops can be conducted at conceptual stages as well as detailed design stages. A detailed report of decisions taken is typically created and that gets incorporated into the value-for-money report where appropriate.

Value Delivery

Value delivery is inherent within a program of work or specific project delivery. Output from value engineering workshops sets the scope parameters for each program of work or project. Further changes may take place during the value delivery stage and classic change control methods should be utilized to "control" value that was locked in at approval time. However, the ability to influence or increase value within the delivery cycle decreases with each successive stage of the value management cycle, similar to the elements of risk (i.e., the closer to the delivery point for outputs, the harder it is to influence, change, or increase value without incurring extra cost). The note of caution here is that proposed changes to scope, either addition or subtraction, during the delivery period require careful analysis, which must include focusing on the operational and life cycle impacts rather than a focus on just cost, time, and scope, which is so often applied.

Value Capture

Value capture can be thought of as a form of benefits realization in that after the delivery of each initiative, be it a program of work or a specific project, value is gathered. In a value management environment, value can be gained toward the end of the value delivery stage as well during the value capture stage. Often, value has a progressive aspect that sees value accumulating as the stages of the value management life cycle are completed. The quality of the effort expended during the value planning stage, as well the decision making associated with controlling the delivery of agreed-upon scope, will greatly enhance the amount of value realized during the value capture period.

In many cases, the full value may not be achieved until well after the delivery of program or project outputs. Therefore, the actual benefits to be gained require careful thought and need to have well-defined and agreed-upon metrics. For straightforward financial metrics, the monetary cost would be accumulated over the life cycle of the initiative and then compared to the overall cost invested.

It is quite conceivable that an enterprise portfolio management office (EPMO) could provide a value capture service to the organization, as long as the EPMO is at a level of maturity where it operates at a true portfolio management level and is staffed by people with high levels of capability, competence, and business acumen. It is also conceivable that a program management office (PMO) could provide a similar supporting service.

Toward the end of the value capture period, a final report should be prepared, which captures relevant information that can be used to affirm that the planned value is fully achieved. This report can also incorporate other content that would provide quality data for use in future strategic and portfolio planning. Similar to program of work and project management, a lessons learned statement, which captures lessons gained from the value capture phase or the overall value management cycle, would also be useful as input toward future value and portfolio planning. A combination of those two would be optimal.

Value Management Framework Summary

In summary, a value management framework used as part of a mature approach to portfolio management will add a great deal of certainty to any series of planned investments (i.e., portfolios). This applies to both internal and external investments. The introduction of a value management framework requires careful planning, as it must be integrated with other enterprise approaches and should incorporate techniques such as business planning, sensitivity analysis, investment logic mapping, program/project delivery, and benefits realization. A value management framework is also a complete mechanism that will provide executives and senior managers with more confidence in investment decisions of any size by dovetailing into what I term *true portfolio management* (i.e., "This is how we do business"). This blends opex and capex investments into a more holistic and more efficient approach. It should also provide greater confidence in responding to the market mantras of "doing more for less" and "faster, better, cheaper."

Portfolio management provides the mechanism to identify a viable and balanced mix of long-term and short-term initiatives for organizational investment. Portfolio management is slowly being recognized as an effective and pragmatic approach to constructing and aligning plans of operational activity, both in a new investment manner and in a BAU manner. However, in order to avoid the process-heavy approaches often seen today, portfolio management must focus on two core aspects:

1. The translation of strategy into actionable plans using a value management framework as the overarching philosophy and mechanism; and
2. Assisting the organization in doing the right things, both in a capital expenditure (capex) and operational expenditure (opex) manner, and balancing them.

These aspects provide a comprehensive view of an organization's intent, direction, and progress, all of which are expressed via portfolios of work. For further proof, here are the top five reasons for this movement toward portfolio management, based on recent research by the Project Management Institute:

- Customer satisfaction,
- Revenue growth,
- Improved return on investment (ROI),
- Reduced development costs, and
- Cost reduction.

Despite the compelling nature of the above benefits, portfolio management that is deployed into the organization as a process-oriented solution will fail simply because it is not balanced, loses executive support, and thereby is not robust enough. Portfolio management that uses a value management framework provides the balance and rigor necessary to inform and assist the organizational planners and decision makers to align all planned activity to the organization's strategic business objectives, and ultimately, its strategic goals. Program of work management executes the planned portfolios and delivers outcomes that are critical for value capture or the realization of benefits within the available investment and resource parameters. Project management executes and delivers outputs for individual projects within a program of work or otherwise. It should be noted, though, that some legacy BAU will exist in the form of business support functions, such as human resources (HR), payroll, finance, and IT support/helpdesk. Section 2 offers details on portfolio management, which is powered by value management. Section 3 offers details and guidance on the management of programs of work and projects.

So, in summary, strategic impact is created when the midterm goals and objectives of an organization are directly connected to groups of portfolios, which are in turn executed via program of work and project initiatives. By using value-driven portfolio management techniques, any organization gains the alignment, impact, and higher visibility of progress toward planned organizational goals and objectives. Better impact usually equates to better business performance!

1-3. Organizational Maturity

Assessing the Maturity of Organizational Performance

For organizations to get truly ahead and meet the challenges set by the post-GFC market requires leaders to assess their organization's ability and readiness to change and adopt new and different ways of conducting business. In terms of economic climates, project-based management is of critical importance, as it delivers value to the organization in both buoyant and downturn times, where time to market and efficient use of available funds and resources are the keys to success. It is of little surprise, then, that the awareness of portfolio and program management is increasing rapidly as organizations take a more holistic view of project management. This appears to be a universal trend and is seen in all sectors, both in the nonprofit and for-profit environments. Today, more and more leaders of organizations are seeking, and in some cases insisting, that more mature project-based management techniques be used to ensure efficient achievement of organizational goals and business objectives. However, it doesn't just happen!

There are two critical factors that contribute to the success of the above, and these, if focused on and executed well, will lay a foundation for success that is sustainable over a reasonable period of time. These critical factors are:

1. Organizational capability and maturity in portfolio, program, and project management (P3M); and
2. Capabilities and skills of people in the organization.

The P3M capability and maturity factor requires an organization to be fully aware of its ability and capability to perform and deliver any portfolio, program, or project successfully, from initiation through to completion and beyond. Making sure that existing skill sets are known and mapped to the program of work and project type and scale is vital, as are the methodologies used to execute each initiative. The maturity also requires robust and appropriate project governance to be evident and in use. This includes leadership and ownership, organizational structure, commercial approaches, and decision making plus macro-change control. No initiative should commence without a business case that clearly demonstrates the value in terms of the output (project deliverable) and the outcome (business benefit) of the proposed initiative. More on organizational maturity is offered in Section 1-6.

In regard to the second critical factor, too often we see the development of talent management restricted to budget-controlled discretionary amounts. Mixed line management and HR views often lead to money being squandered on personalized training. Rather, skills and knowledge development should be part of a defined career path, which contributes directly to the mission of the organization.

Looking toward the future, we shall see much more alignment of portfolio, program, and project management techniques to support the established project management methods that exist today. However, in order to continue to reduce risk of failure of complex projects, organizations must use phased approaches and be crystal clear on where each proposed initiative fits into the organization's business plan, and how it maps to specific business objectives. As the focus on the above-mentioned critical factors continues, organizations, particularly buyers, should develop more incentive-based agreements that drive a culture of success across the supply chain, for mutual benefits rather than the "us and them" approaches that are so often utilized.

The bottom line is to develop your talent to allow your organization to achieve a performance lift that combats complexity, is sustainable, and contributes directly to increased performance. Section 4 contains guidance on talent development via qualifications and credentials.

1-4. Organizational Structure and Design

Organizations are usually structured to address their desired, often short-term, business outcomes. An organization's structure generally falls within one of three categories: functional, matrix, or projectized.

During the 20th century, the functional model was by far the most dominant structure that was established and utilized. It allowed vast benefits and wealth to be gained by having order, discipline, and structure not too dissimilar to an old military style of model. So, although there was success for the post–Industrial Revolution era, today those functional structures are choking and distracting, thereby restricting the ability to adapt.

Looking forward, organizations will need to be more flexible with more empowerment and more cross-functional team working. The notion of the matrix structure has long been around, albeit generally restricted to academic debate and not well practiced in real life. With maturity beginning to rise in program of work and project management, it is now the right time to empower teams much further and speed up organizations by adopting a form of matrix structure.

The following comments and examples on the three categories of structure are provided for consideration.

Functional Structure

Figure 1-3 shows a simplified version of the "classic" structure, where skills are contained within static business functions (or silos), such as design, finance, sales, and so forth. Any cross-functional type of work, such as projects, has to move from one function to another as the various stages are carried out. This can be effective for repetitive, operational tasks, but requires bureaucratic processes and a large overhead to manage. In a program of work/project environment, it can lead to delays and to communication breakdown.

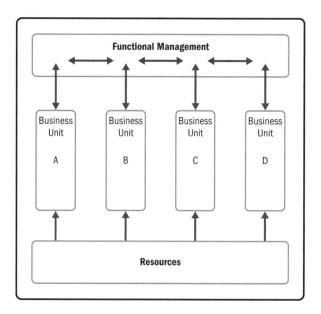

Figure 1-3: Functional structure (simplified).

Matrix Structures

A matrix structure is normally depicted by two axes, often labeled "project" (sometimes "product") and "function" (sometimes "resource"). Dimensions of both axes exercise defined levels of control over the tasks performed and the resources utilized.

The differences lie in the degree of emphasis on functional or project responsibility. The weak matrix is closer to the functional organization, whereas the balanced or strong matrix is closer to a pure team-based projectized organization. In all cases, the accountabilities and responsibilities must be clear, including the establishment of P3M governance models (e.g., steering committees, executive sponsors, etc.).

The following shows examples of three recognizable forms of matrix structure, along with some key points on each:

Weak Matrix

In the weak matrix (Figure 1-4), program of work/project resources *remain* in their business units and report to the functional managers. Progression of program of work/project activities is coordinated by the coordinator function.

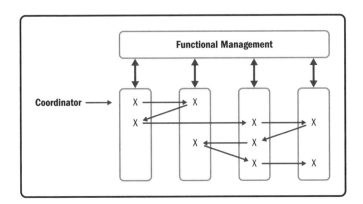

Figure 1-4: Weak matrix.

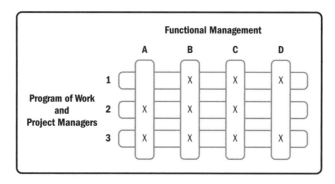

Figure 1-5:   Balanced matrix.

Balanced Matrix

In the balanced matrix (Figure 1-5), program of work and project resources are *seconded* and report directly to program of work/project managers for the duration of each initiative.

Strong Matrix

In the strong matrix (Figure 1-6), program of work and project resources are *dedicated* and report directly to program of work/project managers on a daily basis.

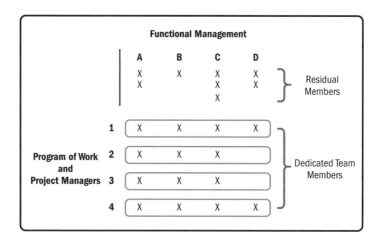

Figure 1-6:   Strong matrix.

Projectized Structure

This form, a variation of the strong matrix, shows that all work is achieved through portfolios, programs of work, and projects. This clearly requires a portfolio-driven culture, where the organization is seeking to better integrate its functions in order to reduce cost, gain efficiency, and maximize profits and competitiveness. In order to do this, many organizations are looking for guidance to move from a functional setup to a more projectized structure. A truly projectized organization operates without any specific functions—rather, it may have a series of portfolios run by cross-functional teams. This option, to be sustainable, requires the organization, and perhaps even the sector it operates within, to have high levels of P3M maturity.

Case Study Example

A good example of this type of approach is that of the W.L. Gore & Associates, Inc. organization, globally known for its Gore-Tex® product range. Following adoption and adaptation, they state: "There are no traditional organizational structures, no chains of command, nor predetermined channels of communication. Instead, we communicate directly with each other and are accountable to fellow members of our multicultural teams."

This clearly works, as W.L. Gore & Associates, Inc. is a global organization that has a wide product range across a diverse market. It employs more than 10,000 people and constantly gets listed in the World Best Multinational Workplaces list by the Great Place to Work® Institute. It was number three in 2016. Furthermore, in 2016, the organization was listed at number 12 in the Fortune 100 Best Companies to Work For®. Their website contains an impressive list of awards and distinctions, which highlights the fact that the right structure and right people together form an appealing culture.

The culture statement is appealing for its simplicity, but also for the assumed levels of trust and empowerment provided to various leaders and their teams.

Company founder Bill Gore articulated four guiding principles that today's associates (they do not use the term *employee*) are still encouraged to adhere to. These are:

- Fairness to each other and everyone with whom we come in contact.
- Freedom to encourage, help, and allow other associates to grow in knowledge, skills, and scope of responsibility.
- The ability to make one's own commitments and keep them.
- Consultation with other associates before undertaking actions that could impact the reputation of the company.

These four value statements require maturity and high levels of judgment to exist and be applied on a daily basis. This is a great example of a culture that would support a value-driven portfolio management approach.

Models on a Continuum

The matrix model that an organization selects will relate to its level of organizational P3M maturity and to the level and complexity of the programs of work it undertakes. The continuum, shown as Figure 1-7, suggests that the more complex and the more specialized the programs of work and projects being planned, the more likely a strong matrix or projectized structure will be required. The key to success, therefore, is to design the organization's structure in a manner that supports the notion of integrated planning, so that the risk of getting lost in the chaos of competing goals, deadlines, and resources becomes manageable. Having well-considered plans, plus enhanced levels of empowerment, enables leaders to speed up decision making within known parameters of authority and the risk that is inherent within each portfolio.

Also, it is important to be honest about your organization's capability level in relation to proposed new investments that are

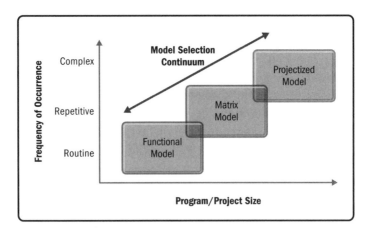

Figure 1-7: Models on a continuum.

larger or more complex than what the organization and its talent are capable of delivering efficiently. Unfortunately, the world is littered with failed initiatives that have had low levels of P3M capability at their core.

1-5. Organizational P3M Governance

P3M governance is the function of creating and using an overarching framework to align, organize, and execute initiatives in a collectively coherent and intelligible manner in order to meet organizational goals and business objectives.

Organizational governance bodies should foster and actively support P3M governance to excite and stimulate the culture required for portfolio-driven activity. Governance of portfolio and program of work activity is similar to the oversight role conducted by those on organizational boards of directors in that it is handsoff from the day-to-day work associated with P3M output and outcome delivery. Therefore, there can be more than one governance method used within an organization. The commonality is in the framework, where pillars of governance revolve around purpose, culture, accountability, and compliance. These equally apply to

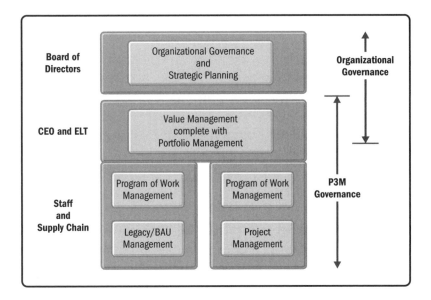

Figure 1-8: Organizational and P3M governance relationships.

corporate governance and to P3M governance. Furthermore, the focus of each must center on existing value protection, value enhancement, and new value creation.

P3M governance is most commonly seen via steering committee, sponsor, and independent quality assurance (IQA) activity. Each governance entity should be consistent yet appropriate to its level of focus. The following, along with Figure 1-8, is offered as guidance to aid the development of multitiered P3M governance models within any organization:

- Create a culture at the top of the organization that has value management as its core mechanism.
- Establish the limits of authority (power), rules of conduct, and protocols of work that organizations/teams can use effectively to advance strategic goals and objectives and to realize anticipated value.
- Seek to fully integrate portfolio management that is supported with programs of work and project management delivery mechanisms.

- Have P3M governance occuring at different decision-making levels of the organization.
- Involve establishing well-developed frameworks with sufficient control mechanisms (e.g., phase/stage gates, review meetings, and approved metrics to monitor progress, etc.).
- Include a strong and mature EPMO that provides high levels of capability and support.

1-6. Organizational Maturity Models

Organizational P3M maturity can be defined as the degree to which an organization practices portfolio, program of work, and project management—sometimes referred to as organizational project management.

Several organizational assessment frameworks have been developed, whereby the organization can be assessed against criteria to determine its maturity level. Included for guidance is an overview of some selected frameworks that provide levels of:

- Explicit criteria to measure performance;
- Benchmarks for an organization (or individual) globally and by industry;
- Identification of areas where improvements may be required; and
- Provision of a basis from which to develop an improvement program and continual assessment mechanism.

4-P Methodology™

Developed by Project Plus Ltd. to provide a pragmatic and wide-reaching system that allows a balanced assessment of an organization's current state of P3M capabilities, the 4-P Methodology™ has, as the name suggests, four focus areas: policy, people, process, and performance. An assessment and subsequent analysis is benchmarked against an international standard and results are stored in a database. The database material can also be used to benchmark practices across geographies and sectors. It can also be used to select across programs of work and project management.

Project Plus Ltd. also offers its Compass Assessment Method™ system that uses a 180-degree review of capability and performance and a comprehensive interview to prepare a detailed development report on an organization's key people.

Both systems can lead to a strategic road map of change being built. Each road map is integrated and time planned to enhance success and reduce risk of failure to the organization.

Capability Maturity Model (CMM) Overview

Developed by the Software Engineering Institute of Carnegie-Mellon University in the United States between 1986 and 1993, and arguably the most recognized model, this model's premise is that an organization advances through a series of five stages of primarily process maturity. The classic five-level scale is utilized to reflect a maturity level. The levels are summarized as follows:

> **Level 1 – Initial:** Ad hoc process, no adequate guidance, no consistency.
> **Level 2 – Repeatable:** Process depends on individuals, minimum of process controlling guidance exists, high risk for new challenges.
> **Level 3 – Defined:** Process defined and institutionalized, process groups defined.
> **Level 4 – Managed:** Process is quantitatively measured, metrics for quality and productivity exist, collection of process and experience.
> **Level 5 – Optimizing:** Continual improvement of process, continual collection of data to identify improvements, analysis of defects for prevention.

Furthermore, as organizations mature, their programs and project performance improve and become more predictable and controlled, and therefore present lower risk of failure to the organization.

Four Quadrant (4Q) Assessment

The 4Q model has been developed and is owned by Human Systems International. They claim to have the largest global database of material that represents P3M practices built over a 20-year period. These practices are shared with member organizations in various forums around the world. Based on a foundation of corporate culture, the model is built around the following four segments:

- Process Assessment – approach,
- Practice Assessment – deployment,
- Talent Management – assessment, and
- Portfolio Characterization – assessment.

The material in the database is used to benchmark practices across geographies and sectors and also across portfolio, program, and project management.

Organizational Project Management Maturity Model (OPM3®)

OPM3® is a maturity model from the Project Management Institute (PMI) that has three interlocking elements, namely, knowledge, assessment, and improvement.

The model is designed to align organization strategy and execution so that project outputs contribute toward organizational success.

OPM3® assesses best practices achieved within areas of portfolio management, program management, and project management. This is measured via four stages of process improvement:

- Standardize—acquire knowledge,
- Measure—perform assessment,
- Control—manage improvement, and
- Continuously improve—repeat the cycle.

Portfolio, Program, and Project Management Maturity Model (P3M3)

Originally developed by the United Kingdom Office of Government and Commerce (OGC), but now in the stewardship of AXELOS, a form of public-private partnership entity based in the United Kingdom, P3M3 is focused on the review of seven process groups. The model offers a self-assessment version that allows an organization to conduct its own internal reviews as well as predict its likely level of maturity. An enhanced version allows for baselining across five levels of maturity. There is a risk of subjectivity associated with internal reviews, which potentially lowers the value of the model.

1-7. The 3 Ps to Success

Adoption of refined and mature approaches to what is often termed *organizational project management* can offer leaders a solution to the challenges they may be facing. The solution, again though, must be an integrated one, which requires careful planning and passionate belief to be successfully implemented and full benefits to be gained. The solution revolves around a simplified model herein called *the 3 Ps to Success*. This is wider than the common process-oriented aspects of some of the models discussed in Section 1-6, but keeps the implementation pragmatic to drive and gain results faster via improvement. The elements of the 3 Ps to Success model are as follows:

- **Purpose** – setting strategy and policy relating to that strategy, related critical success factors (CSFs), goals and objectives, and linkages to P3M governance. There should also be strong views and focus on culture embedded in this element. These cultural elements would need to be triggered, owned, and actively supported by the governance levels of the organization (e.g., board of directors and executive managers). The adoption of value management as an overarching framework drives portfolio management adoption and the translation of strategic intentions and objectives into actionable plans.

- **People** – building from the purpose statement and recognizing that it is the people connected to the organization that truly make the difference. Recognizing that strong empowerment of people through well-defined accountability and responsibility frameworks is critical for success. Also, skill development and experiential learning will allow people to use their head, heart, and gut to make better decisions much faster than any process-centric method hopes to achieve.
- **Performance** – maintaining a focus on driving for results is key here. This would include a system of organizational performance management for reviewing and guiding toward multiple success points via CSF trending, program key performance indicators (KPIs), and project output data. This would also include the affirmation of business benefits being realized post–program of work and after project delivery. The balancing of opex with capex to produce an integrated business plan would also be integrated.

The mechanism to deliver this type of model is via an organization-wide cultural change initiative. It is not, and should never be, via mundane process-driven change management approaches that unfortunately we see too often. We need more of what I term *passionate change* of all types that is integrated and operates at all levels of the organization.

In the beginning of the "new age of simplicity," I would encourage you as a leader and reader of this book to finds ways to utilize the 3 Ps to Success philosophy in a manner that is simple to deploy and becomes contagious as a result.

1-8. The Modern Lean Organization

Over the previous decades, there have been many business management models offered, with most, if not all, claiming to be the best. No doubt, there will be those that continue to offer new or varied ways to run an organization successfully and sustainably. Of those that have emerged, some have had their "day in the sun" for a period before being superseded by the latest or "next best thing" model. A bit of reflection on some of those models suggests that they were often very process centric and, until recently, very process heavy. This has resulted in organizations becoming process choked and focusing more on compliance than on getting things done in a better manner that excites clients/customers along the way.

Other personal observations suggest the "copycat" management style, where some organizational leaders simply, or at least seemed to, copy the adoption of these models from a competitor or other organization with little consideration of their suitability to the current organization. Common practice is best practice, right? Not necessarily!

The future of operational management must focus on the need for nimbleness together with speed and effectiveness within a framework of acceptable risk thresholds. Adopting a philosophy of lean, not necessarily "lean enterprise," is a critical first consideration. Next is to build a culture around the 3 Ps to Success and value management together with portfolio management. These will allow the organization to speed up, reduce waste, and be more readily adaptable to future change opportunities. Start with your culture and blend it with the other aspects associated with establishing/renewing your organization's purpose. Follow that by introducing a value management framework while adopting portfolio management to suit.

This means a considerable change in structure and in culture. The objective is for a "passion for change and opportunity" to emerge as a cultural mantra, which becomes sustainable by being adopted wholeheartedly throughout the organization. It also means a considerable investment in the people within the organization. In the future, leaders will need to delegate much more than they currently do. More decision making on the front line of operations will work, but only if those front-line staff are given the right training, coaching, and guidance regarding policy frameworks to empower them to develop and foster an exciting culture. An exciting culture is one that uses the 3 Ps to Success as the platform for engagement and for success—that is, a well-communicated, clear purpose; empowered people in a matrix structure; and a performance-driven focus on what is really important (e.g., critical success factors). It also has strong value statements that are extrapolated from the 3 Ps to Success.

1-9. Talent Management

The war for talent is heating up again after abating for a while during and following the global financial crisis. A recent survey by the London-based Economist Intelligence Unit (EIU) that queried almost 600 C-suite executives from around the world gives cause for concern when 72% stated that their organizational performance had suffered because of a lack of necessary skills. When you have CEOs, CFOs, CIOs, and COOs stating this, there are issues with the current skills on offer versus the future skills that are required. This is more than a resource capacity problem in terms of volume of people available to do work. The gap highlights a significant shift in the skills necessary to complete work that is more becoming complex.

As the global economy slowly recovers and a so-called "new normal" takes hold, organizations are seeking to regain competitive advantage or efficiency gains by doing more project-based work that focuses on core business. On the face of it, this is great; however, some research by global consultancy KPMG suggests that these organizations are committing to a higher volume of projects that are significantly more complex and that require more money to finance. These factors must dramatically increase the risk of failure at an organizational level and the potential brand damage through lack of resources with the right skill set. Going back to the EIU survey, the lack of skills suggests there is a problem looming, especially when another part of the same survey found that the most important individual skill those executives identified was the ability to "get stuff done," and the most important organizational capability was "finding leaders to implement strategic change." One conclusion we can draw from this is that future talent will need to acquire or develop advanced skills to deal with increasing complexity and volume of work while balancing risk and exploiting opportunity within established thresholds.

Global Hunt for Talent

The surge in demand for talent will see organizations throughout the world (including those in emerging economies), via their national governments, hunt globally for talent that has the key capabilities to get stuff done quickly. This could drain existing skill sets and in turn create shortages within those countries from which the talent comes. For example, rebuilding the city of Christchurch in New Zealand has taken considerably longer than desired, not because of funding restrictions, but as a result of shortages of various skill sets that are required.

There are two further changes emerging within the wider talent pool that should concern those in the boardrooms, the executive offices, and the HR departments of all organizations: the massive amount of talent retirement and the increasing transient nature of the next generation workforce.

Data from the United Nation's Population Division titled "World Population Prospects on Retirement Age Populations" show dramatic increases in people reaching retirement age over the next couple of decades. In New Zealand, it is anticipated that 25% of the population will be age 65 or more in 2050. Another, albeit anecdotal, example from a CEO was that within the next five to 10 years, 50% of the existing talent pool from the global oil and gas sector will be at retirement age.

While current workforce talent is being tempted overseas, presumably to pursue better opportunities, future workforce generations will be far more mobile than current ones. Resources of tomorrow will move from job to job more often and quickly, as their whim and/or need dictates. We see the beginnings of this today. Individuals and teams can research, consider, and act on job vacancies from anywhere in the world. Those individuals will make engagement decisions that include factors other than just monetary-based reward systems. Social networking and informal referrals will lead much of this activity. For example, you might get a group of young skilled professionals who are geographically spread networking via Facebook asking, "Is this organization cool?" or "Can we contract for three or four months to raise some cash for our next trip?" Workforce loyalty will take on an entirely different meaning for those "global gypsies" on the go.

Pressure to Attract and Retain

As a consequence of the above, there will be pressure on an organization's ability to attract and retain resources that have the skills for the future economies in sufficient capacity (i.e., getting stuff done and leading strategic change). Shortages in skilled resources will cause organizations to create more contract opportunities, with many of those in a project-based environment. Those organizations that leverage professional online recruitment and social media tools, such as LinkedIn, should benefit from access to skilled resources in different areas of the world.

So, other than simply retaining the pending retirees for longer, what must organizations do to convince and attract those skilled global gypsies to set up camp and stay a while? The answer lies in organizations making themselves as attractive as they can be to those people. This is more than branding or marketing. The attraction needs to be multifaceted and clearly demonstrate elements of excitement and empowerment, development opportunities, career path options, and entrepreneurial extras. All this needs to be conveyed through different technologies that reach this highly mobile and tech-savvy group of global gypsies. This will also require those organizations to make additional budget provisions for more elaborate reward and retention programs that go beyond traditional bonus-type systems. A useful starting point is to fully define what skills are important to the organization and then understand the current capabilities of existing resources, and thereby the organization itself. By conducting capability assessments on existing talent, organizations will gain a clear capability picture of that talent, which can then be compared to future talent requirements (remember: more projects, greater complexity, and bigger budgets) and gaps identified. Developmental investment can then be targeted, better career paths established, and volume increased through recruitment.

Restructuring the organization to a balanced matrix type should make it more attractive for those seeking relatively short-term project-type opportunities. A balanced matrix would allow future work to be better packaged for execution via project-based approaches. This facilitates a deeper team culture and shared objectives that create highly functioning teams, as per author Patrick Lencioni, where trust, unfiltered conflict around ideas, commitment, and accountability all lead to the better achievement of collective results. Emotional intelligence and emotional quadrant skills will become more prominent. Executive and senior management levels will need to gain new skills that support P3M governance and the deployment and empowerment of teams that convene together for a given purpose and period and then disband once deliverables are confirmed.

Rather than operate as another level of management structure, perhaps professional directors and their boards need to focus more on the organization's vision, goals, and culture; communicate those clearly and wholeheartedly; and proactively support the achievement of that vision. If boards can focus on crafting the strategic direction from their vision, then the management levels can deploy portfolio, program, and project management approaches, supported with effective governance and development of new skills, to achieve the vision. This will create strategic alignment throughout the organization while maintaining maximum flexibility and nimbleness to adjust as needs require.

A Cool Place To Be

A fully projectized approach to organizational structures allows for faster achievement of strategy while maximizing the relatively short availability of scarce skilled resources. The organization becomes a "cool" place to be for a while, as it offers talent more opportunities to work on projects that are time bound, stimulating, creative, and possibly well rewarded.

It could be argued that business in the Western world is more focused on compliance and reduction of liability with further layers of political correctness. These attributes lead to compromise and the "watering down" of vision and associated budgets rather than fostering creativity, excitement, and fun—attributes that are likely to make an organization more appealing to the global gypsy talent pool. To be successful, organizations must adopt different approaches to attracting and retaining skilled resources that are becoming increasingly migratory in nature.

Governments should create better policy that maintains democracy, yet balances sustainability, reduces/eliminates political correctness, welcomes and embraces creativity, and reduces compromise. In addition, they should review policies to improve access to skilled workforces and business migration visas. If this is done, we should witness better retention of resources within the geographical boundaries of the country as the business environment becomes more dynamic.

How Can Talent Risks Be Mitigated and Managed?

Every organization needs to look well ahead and relate talent demand to its strategic and operational plans. This talent demand look ahead should use portfolio management techniques that focus on enabling, capacity, balancing, and prioritization of resources within the plans. The following seven-point risk mitigation plan should assist in:

- Building your brand so it's talked about as cool;
- Conducting capability assessments;
- Conducting better talent needs analysis;
- Recruiting for success—provide incentive package and build good relationships;
- Targeting and bringing back previous employees who have left the organization;
- Positioning post or second people as part of their career path; and
- Creating a 10- to 15-year HR plan.

Talent Management Summary

The bottom line is that organizations of all sizes need to have human talent management on their key corporate risk list, or at least on their priority list. Organizations need to focus on and invest in making their brand really attractive and modify policies and processes for better resource development and utilization. People talent is no longer an HR department issue; it's an organizational risk that requires proactive attention by all leaders and managers.

1-10. Organizational Risks

For those who have to consider and deal with organizational risk on a regular basis, the challenge is growing considerably and quickly. There is no question that today's risks, in their many forms, are challenging board members, executives, managers, and those involved in the P3M profession. In fact, a 2016 global survey of C-suite and senior leaders by accounting and advisory firm BDO found that 87% of respondents believe that the world has become a riskier place. No surprise really, when one looks at the news headlines on any given day.

Wise leaders probably already know that increasing risk is usually derived from some form of change. However, where there is risk there is also opportunity. So, what does this mean for today's leaders? Well, it means greater vigilance and a proactive manner are essential. In other words, we need to be vigilant and forward thinking when it comes to risk management, but equally we need to balance how we capitalize on business opportunities that present themselves. To get ahead or even to stay in business or stay relevant, leaders must put renewed attention on risk/opportunity management, starting holistically and integrating down through the organization. Chasing opportunities, even if balanced by good risk management, introduces, more often than not, some form of change. Using portfolio, program of work, and project-based approaches will greatly assist, as the P3M profession already has a good grounding and track record on managing risk and capitalizing on opportunity through "getting stuff done."

Earlier in this section, we discussed the value management framework as an overarching approach to linking strategic intent and plans with operational activity via portfolio management techniques. These blended approaches will allow for a more integrated and balanced insight into risks/opportunities, particularly around the interdependencies of risks and the maximization of value capture across well-developed plans that are aligned to the goals and objectives of the organization.

A value-driven portfolio management approach will allow you to facilitate a higher-level, integrated, and constructive dialogue to take place at various levels in the boardroom, the office of the CEO, and throughout the organization, and especially in EPMOs that are focusing on portfolio management from both the opex and capex perspectives.

How is this done? It begins with establishing the right culture across the organization as part of the 3 Ps to Success. This is a culture that sees risk and opportunity as methods that enhance decision making and option taking in a consistent and sustainable manner. This culture must be holistic across its deployment and must be linked to all activity within the organization. The culture would consider thresholds, openness, compliance, and opportunity investment. Core principles would be based on preserving relevant existing value, creating new value, and seeking future value. A framework that encompasses those elements must be available to all staff to use and effect. It should be noted that the commentary so far focuses on what is termed *business risk,* as opposed to *pure risk.* The major difference is that business risk has a loss or gain aspect to it, whereas pure risk has only a loss. The organization's ability to deal with pure risk is quite limited, whereas it has a greater ability to deal with business risk, which includes an opportunity element, if it is set up for it from the boardroom down through the organizational hierarchy.

In dealing with risk and opportunity, organizations need to consider both the internal and external risks it is or believes itself to be exposed to. These groupings can be used formally or informally to offset the risks or capitalize on the opportunities. We can then apply or consider risk types that allow us to focus on a particular risk or group of risks that may have similar characteristics. Examples of risk types and associated characteristics include:

- Technical – scope related, complexity, volume, cyber, performance;
- Financial – funding, cash flow, profitability;
- Commercial – environmental, schedule (timings), contract/legal, supply chain;
- Resource – capabilities, volume, sources, costs; and
- Corporate – merger and acquisition, transformation, nimbleness, culture, brand perception;

No organization, whether for profit or nonprofit, can stand still and not make decisions regarding risk. However, an organization can manage its risks by elevating and integrating risk in a scalable manner across all its business activity. The benefits gained from the active and mature use of risk management across all portfolio-driven activity are huge. In addition to cost and time drivers and targets, client perception and brand reputation will lift, thereby grossly affecting both perceived and actual value.

In a portfolio management environment, business results can be enhanced by minimizing risks and capitalizing on opportunities much earlier, which can save cost. Another clear benefit is that teams working on any initiative should have a more satisfying experience as a result of less stress and tension caused by "firefighting" operational issues. It is critical, then, that the leaders of any organization develop sound risk policy, which must include thresholds and ensure that the policy is well understood and used by everyone in the organization. This is not just about compliance, which is mandatory, but advocating for a positive proactiveness that allows the organization to move quickly and efficiently when it needs to.

As more global trade, networking, and other alliances form, more disruptive technologies come into effect, and the risk of not doing anything different becomes significant. The solution path is to build around the 3 Ps to Success, adopt a value management framework, and have the confidence to deploy true portfolio management; this is how we do business.

*Every day do something that will inch
you closer to a better tomorrow.*

—**Doug Firebaugh**

Portfolio Management: A Way of Doing Business

2-1. The Rise of Portfolio Management

Portfolio management is now being recognized as an effective and pragmatic approach to aligning and connecting strategy-based plans with actual organizational activity. Indeed, the International Organization for Standardization (ISO) has recently released a standard for portfolio management—ISO 21504. This is part of the ISO 21000 series on portfolio, program, and project management. Portfolio management can apply both in a new investment manner and in a "business as usual" manner. Although it has its roots in project-based management, portfolio management has borrowed some of the philosophy from the finance sector, particularly around grouping and commonality. These groupings now provide a viable and pragmatic business management mechanism for the implementation of strategic plans. The lack of an effective mechanism has long been an area that has troubled executives and senior managers in their quest for efficient and effective operational and tactical activity that aligns to their strategic plans. When portfolio management is coupled together with value management, particularly the value management framework, outlined in Section 1-2, a very real mechanism results that positions portfolios at the right level to assist those involved in strategy/business planning. This avoids the common risk of a portfolio management framework becoming process heavy, which chokes the organization and lessens the perceived value it offers. I often refer to this trend as the "book of rules," or the "book of theory" mentality.

2-2. High-Level View of Portfolio Management

A portfolio is a collection of components that have some form of planned investment that meets strategic business objectives. For example, a portfolio can be made up of programs of work, projects, and other work, such as maintenance and ongoing operations. All those are grouped together to facilitate effective and efficient execution of the work.

At least one portfolio should exist within an organization typically comprising a set of current prioritized initiatives that are executed using some form of program of work or project management techniques. These initiatives may or may not be related, interdependent, or even managed as a portfolio. This offers a good deal of flexibility to those planning as well as to those implementing the portfolio.

Figure 2-1 shows a high-level example of portfolios and their relationships with programs of work, projects, and other work. It hints at a (sometimes) complex relationship among these components. This may or not apply to you, as each organization adapts to its specific circumstances.

All components of a portfolio will typically exhibit common features, such as:

- They are aligned with the organization's strategy and linked to its identified goals and objectives;
- They represent investments via budget allocations made or intended by the organization;

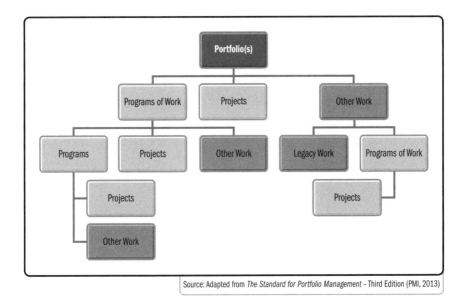

Source: Adapted from *The Standard for Portfolio Management* - Third Edition (PMI, 2013)

Figure 2-1:   Portfolio management high-level view.

- They typically have one or more distinguishing features that prompt the organization to group them for more efficient management and control purposes;
- The components are quantifiable—that is, they can be ranked, prioritized, and measured; and
- They should look to include relevant BAU-related work.

To be valued as an organizational performance contributor, each portfolio must, as necessary, be overseen by an effective P3M governance structure that is empowered to authorize change to its component makeup. These portfolios are then implemented via program of work and project management–based activity.

The above, together with value management, allows the notion of strategic alignment and impact to actually be demonstrated and achieved. The impact and value of portfolio management becomes obvious as the organization moves toward a culture and practice of "this is the way we do business." The value is derived from portfolio management being hinged to value and being well understood at all levels. It becomes a culture, and creates a positive energy throughout the entire organization.

2-3. Portfolio and Portfolio Management Explained

We should take some time to consider what the terms *portfolio* and *portfolio management* should focus on, as it seems that there is a lot of confusion within organizational leadership as well as throughout the project management profession. The terms *portfolio* and *portfolio management* are relatively recent additions to the project management lexicon, and more so to the business language lexicon. The use of these terms suggests a maturing profession that is seeking to expand its knowledge as well as its influence base. The term *project management* has had a much longer exposure in the workplace and has been in widespread use for decades, thus becoming quite common language in most organizations.

Portfolio

Put simply, a portfolio is "a way of doing business." A portfolio should reflect the total or parts of investment planned or made by an organization. These should be aligned with the organization's strategic goals and business objectives. It's a collection of programs of work, projects, and other work grouped together to facilitate effective governance, management, and control of that work to meet strategic goals and business objectives. The components are quantifiable; they can be measured, ranked, and prioritized. The content of each portfolio may not necessarily be interdependent or directly related, although in practice this is often the case. You are encouraged to maintain this viewpoint in order to provide as much clarity and focus as possible to those involved in implementing.

The portfolio is where priorities are identified, investment decisions are made, capacity is analyzed, and resources (human, financial, etc.) are allocated. If a portfolio's components are not aligned to its organizational objectives, the organization's leaders can reasonably question why the investment is being proposed, its value contribution, or why the work is being undertaken.

Portfolio Management

Portfolio management is the centralized management of one or more portfolios, which includes enabling, identifying, balancing, measuring, adjusting, and reviewing/renewing programs of work, projects, and other work to achieve specific strategic business objectives.

Based on this, and the earlier definition of portfolios being "a way of doing business," portfolio management is quite different from program of work management, project management, or other management disciplines. These differences are mostly around the level of focus, in that portfolio management considers the achievement of goals and objectives at a strategic level, while programs of work, projects, and other work are focused on the achievement of specific outputs and outcomes—a form of subplan.

Portfolio Management Office

A portfolio management office is a management structure that is usually established to support the creation and execution of one or more portfolios.

It is suggested that in order to keep things relatively simple, it is best to have a single portfolio management office, often referred to as an EPMO, where the E stands for "enterprise." The portfolio management office/EPMO has a strategic and overall business performance focus. Other, sometimes smaller, portfolio management offices may be created elsewhere in the organization to support program of work, project, and BAU activity. Section 4-4 has more on those supporting portfolio management office entities.

A portfolio management office, or EPMO, should work very closely with key business units, such as Finance and those responsible for strategic planning, sometimes referred to as Strategy and Policy. A framework needs to be developed that supports the translation and mapping of strategic desires into portfolios, the high-level control and reporting of portfolios, and also the easy translation and transfer of portfolio content to lower levels for implementation purposes. Key to success here is to identify the key functions of the EPMO and its structure, and to integrate those with other key business units while keeping the framework as light as possible. Resist the temptation to create the "book of rules" or "book of theory" via process-heavy methodologies. The use of a value management framework will greatly assist in the mitigation of that.

2-4. Organizational Context of Portfolio Management

Figure 2-2 shows the general relationships among the strategic and tactical processes within an organization.

From the vision, mission, and other inputs, the organizational strategy, together with goals and objectives, is developed. Implementation of the strategy requires the application of a strategic implementation management process, such as the value management model, supported by appropriate systems and tools, so that high-level planning and management control systems are developed and deployed for implementation purposes.

The top two layers of the pivot model (illustrated in Figure 2-2) set the desired and specific objectives to guide more detailed organizational planning and implementation actions. The middle of the

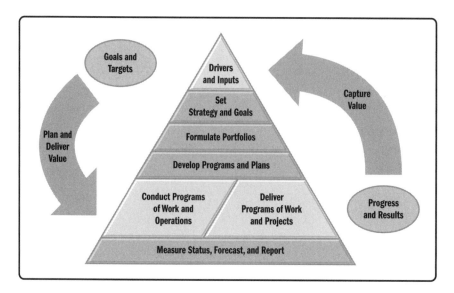

Figure 2-2: The pivot model.

triangle represents the processes that establish portfolios that seek to meet the organizational objectives, and thereby the strategic goals. The bottom of the triangle shows the components that ensure the portfolios are executed effectively and efficiently via program of work, project, and other BAU work. Portfolio management must consider and plan both operational and new investment aspects of the organization so that integrated, balanced, and value-driven output and outcomes drive business performance results.

Portfolio Management Links with Strategy

During the business planning cycle, work components are reviewed and their impact is validated in relation to their alignment with corporate strategy and the perceived value they offer. This is a dynamic and somewhat iterative business planning process that should be part of regular annual planning, or strategic refreshing. Reviews, perhaps six monthly, should lead to possible further refreshing or updates to both the strategy and related business objectives and the associated portfolios. Within this planning cycle, a consistent view of strategic risk would be maintained, which needs to assess the degree of both pure risk (has a negative impact only) and business risk (can have either a positive or negative impact). Other factors that should be considered include value elements, such as:

- Viability of each component that is business case driven;
- Value and its priority and relationship to other investments;
- Available capacity and capability of resources to perform the work; and
- Modifications, additions, and deletions of portfolio components.

The above supports the notion that portfolio management has a rolling-wave nature (i.e., it never ends), whereas program of work and project management have defined start and end points—an incremental and adaptive nature, if you prefer.

Portfolio Management Links with Operations

Legacy operational groups are likely to be stakeholders or perhaps sponsors of portfolio components, such as BAU programs of work. Therefore, portfolio management staff must interact in a constructive and positive way to influence and align various organizational functions, such as the following:

- **Finance:** Tangible, timely, and accurate cost information is required, including return on investment (ROI), profitability, end-cost forecasting, savings prediction, and reserve management. Ideally, this should be a mutual sharing of information between the finance system and the portfolio management system.
- **Human Resources:** The EPMO produces and shares enterprise resource planning to identify the skills and qualifications required, so that a dynamic and relevant resource pool is maintained for deployment on programs of work, specific projects, and other work. Today, individual capability assessments are used more to measure the existing P3M capability of the human resources working on portfolios, programs of work, and projects. These assessment reports usually include suggestions for professional development. Section 4 discusses typical skill sets required for a portfolio management environment. Skills sets for program of work and project management resources are also discussed.
- **Innovation/New Product Development:** Allows and incorporates these critical elements into appropriate portfolios, so that there is consistent balance across the whole organization. Inputs from this area could be triggered from changes seen or anticipated from the market.
- **Marketing:** In essence, this is all about noticing and analyzing "drivers of change," often triggered by an external environment. This would provide data on market analysis, benchmarking, and other pertinent research information as inputs to strategic and value planning.

The analyzed data is required for product or service development, component selection and management, value for money, or value to strategic goals.

- **Procurement:** If your organization has established "preferred supplier" relationships with your supply chain, then it is critical that you consider their capability and capacity to meet your value-driven portfolio management demands. A change to fixed-price incentive contract forms with those preferred suppliers would work particularly well with the balancing of portfolios and the easing of downstream business constraints (e.g., time, cost, benefits, value, etc.) from the programs of work and project implementation activity.

- **Public Relations/Corporate Communications:** In order to maintain stakeholder (internal and external) confidence and support, executives need to regularly communicate and update on strategic progress and any adjustments.

- **Risk and Assurance:** Corporate risk is a big thing to all organizational leaders, and rightly so. Today, there are so many new aspects to risk that the modern world has introduced, with arguably the biggest being brand reputation risk. Risk and assurance leaders must have a clear and full view of risk throughout the whole organization, including its key supply chain partners. Portfolio management will facilitate that view, but also offer more value gains through earlier and better opportunity taking, the oft-forgotten flip side of risk management.

The use of a value management framework will greatly assist those leaders involved to maintain an appropriate level of thinking and decision making toward determining the content of each portfolio. This is achieved by the value management framework allowing for considered, yet timely, responses to the market mantras of "better, faster, cheaper" or "doing more for less," which were commented on in Section 1-1.

Table 2-1:   Key functions comparison table.

Portfolios	Programs of Work	Projects
Focus on business scope that changes with organizational strategic goals and business objectives.	Wide or defined scope; may change to meet benefits expectations of the organization.	Defined scope; specific deliverables as outputs.
Portfolio managers continually monitor changes in the broad environment.	Program managers expect change and embrace it within the confines of the program of work scope.	Project managers focus to minimize and/or control change.
Success is measured in terms of aggregate performance of portfolio components and trends toward strategic business objectives.	Success measured by ROI, new capabilities, and benefits achievement.	Success measured by budget, on time, and deliverables produced to specification, plus customer-specific needs.
Portfolio managers create and maintain necessary frameworks and communication relative to the aggregate portfolios.	Program managers create high-level plans providing guidance to projects and BAU on expected outcomes.	Project and BAU managers conduct detailed planning to manage the delivery of expected outputs.
Portfolio managers monitor and aggregate performance and value indicators across the organization.	Program managers monitor projects and ongoing BAU work within each program of work.	Project managers monitor and control the work of producing each project's deliverables/outputs.

2-5. Comparison of Portfolios, Programs of Work, and Projects

The range of skill sets required for each of the portfolio, program of work, and project roles varies depending on the key functions that each role performs. Table 2-1 provides a sample of some of the typical key functions carried out.

2-6. Interactions and Benefits of Portfolio Management

The term *strategic alignment* suggests that many interactions between portfolios, programs of work, and projects exist. Interactions between portfolio and programs of work typically fall into many categories. These categories and their interactions relate to:

- Initiating each program of work within each portfolio,
- Providing progress data and information to the portfolio domain during each program of work life cycle,
- Facilitating changes to each program of work that are driven from the portfolio domain,

- Formally closing each program of work and related projects, and
- Validating and confirming that the planned and expected benefits are, in fact, achieved.

In summary, portfolio management focuses on "doing the right things." Programs of work and project management traditionally focus on "doing things right." Each offers organizational value through preserving existing value, adding new value, and striving toward the creation of future value. From these, we can gauge the impact and tangible benefits an organization could expect to gain. These would likely include:

- A nimbler organization (i.e., able to adapt and respond quickly to the need for change);
- More efficient use of resources (e.g., human, finance, asset, plant);
- Optimization of resource demand and deployment in the context of each program of work's need for either opex or capex initiative; and
- Faster delivery of incremental (short- and midterm) benefits leading to benefit management sustainability as part of the value management method.

2-7. Introduction to Benefits Management

What is Benefits Management?

This is an interesting question, in that there could be many answers offered, each with some level of appropriateness. This is because, somewhat surprisingly, there is no universal view on what benefits management is. Indeed, there is no universal agreement on the term itself, with *benefits management, benefits realization,* and *business benefits realization* being examples of terms commonly used to mean the same thing. However, benefits management, as we shall call it, is a somewhat revived focus area for executives and senior-level managers who are continuing to look for ways to achieve more for less within their respective organizations. Some research conducted suggests that there are many interpretations and different ways to apply benefits management, with some based on comprehensive key performance indicators, while others are based on detailed process steps. However, a conclusion reached is that benefits management should focus more on integration and completeness of organizational planning and reporting than on measures alone. Therefore, the following interpretation of benefits management is the basis of what is often referred to as "alignment" (i.e., the integration of goals, objectives, initiatives, programs of work, and projects in a model that is as simple as possible, to achieve ease of execution):

> Benefits management is the process of realizing actual outcomes by breaking down strategic business objectives into programs of work and projects, then monitoring the outputs to confirm that the intended benefits have actually been achieved. (Fraser, 2003)

As can be seen, this definition is quite straightforward, and one could expect this to already be practiced across all organizations. To some degree, this is true in that traditional tools such as net present value (NPV), planned value (PV), internal rate of return (IRR), and return on investment (ROI) have formed a financial backbone of organizational planning and measurement, and thereby have offered a form of benefits management. However, new thinking on benefits management extends this financial focus to include the project life cycle and reviews the quality and content of the organizational outcome(s), which normally manifest themselves after the delivery of output from project-based activity.

Characteristics of Benefits Management

We have all seen many management trends/fads come and go over the years. Some have claimed more success than others, whereas others have been excellent examples of "fashionable following." Some examples might include:

- Project management,
- Management by objectives,
- Seven management and planning tools,
- Total quality management (TQM),
- Balanced scorecard (BSC),
- Triple bottom line,
- Portfolio management, and
- Six Sigma.

Those that have lasted through the "latest fashion trending" would include project management, the seven management and planning tools, and benefits management. Benefits management is not new and should not be considered a fad. However, it still is not a universally adopted business management mechanism. Nevertheless, as business and organizational leaders begin to focus on looking further ahead than the next quarter's or the next month's results and beyond traditional financial measures, benefits management techniques allow them to explore the quality of the outcomes from each planned initiative with more confidence and accuracy. In other words, benefits management is a more mature tool, particularly in regard to ongoing investment, that extends the classic project life cycle while synchronizing and integrating through the desired business planning model being used. It is, therefore, more than a short-term trend, as it encourages executives and managers to strategize and plan over a longer-term period. This, at the same time as being able to debate and agree to the perceived value contribution of intended benefits at the time of business case consideration.

Why the Need for Benefits Management?

Around the world, in small and large economies alike, there exists continued pressure within organizations to demonstrate performance, drive value, tie results to measures, and respond quickly to changes, while balancing an internal and external perspective. Internally focused examples of these are an organization's desire for lower risk, competitive advantage, and to make and retain profits and/or improve efficiency. Externally focused examples are based on customers wanting lower cost, wanting faster delivery, and wanting what they expected and agreed to. Therefore, the question that leaders should be trying to answer is:

> How can we measure and communicate our organization-wide performance to ensure that our strategic goals, objectives, critical success factors, and overall mission and purpose are achieved to the satisfaction of our customers, employees, shareholders, and stakeholders? (Fraser, 2003)

As mentioned earlier, the core reason for portfolio management is to link and align actual work done with the strategic intent of the organization. Furthermore, portfolio management should assist in objectively verifying that benefits can be captured through change. The change may be to do things differently, to do different things, or to do things that will influence others to change.

Programs of work typically deliver new or modified capability; the focus of benefits management is on the realization of organizational benefits from this new or modified capability.

Toward the end of each program of work, as individual project initiatives are completed, initial benefits will begin to be realized. However, the realization process will continue because the majority of benefits may not be realized until well after the program of work is completed.

Although benefits management is an area of focus throughout each program of work or project life cycle, it extends beyond the life cycle closure, with ongoing monitoring and review across a nominated and agreed-upon time frame that should be clearly stated in the investment business case.

It is critical to measure the "before" state, so that there is some way of assessing whether the "after" state measurements indicate an improvement (i.e., a benefit gain) or not. It is also critical to keep the benefits management process simple and integrated with other key planning functions, such as the value management framework. This reduces the risk of a process-dominated "book of rules" or "book of theory" being created.

More details on the benefits management process are offered in Section 3-6.

2-8. Portfolio Management Success Factors

To be successful and then sustainable in the use of portfolio management, your organization and its portfolio leaders must:

- Influence and intimately understand the organization's strategic plan and related objectives;
- Use a value management framework as the overarching mechanism to consider and determine each portfolio's content. Use this overarching mechanism to link strategic planning, portfolio planning, and financing together;
- Establish critical success factors and a forward path for determining and managing each portfolio and its direct relationship to one or more of the organization's business objectives;
- Consider all the organization's work needs, including portfolio, programs of work, and project components. Seek to include BAU work in portfolios, so it gets implemented via various programs of work; and
- Satisfy yourselves that the required human capabilities (skill sets) and capacity (volume) are present or easily sourced from an existing supply chain partner or other entity.

Although planning at a business-unit level can produce a desirable output in terms of a multiyear business plan, it is too often not strategic. Frequently, it seems that those plans go wrong because they are not fully planned, communicated, or implemented, which then causes confusion throughout the organization. This means that performance results are not complete in terms of meeting organizational goals or business objectives, or the needs of shareholders and stakeholders. The use of portfolio management guided by a value management framework in a mature manner will result in a business plan that is more holistic, robust, and easier to communicate through the organization and, critically, one that can be focused upon and therefore delivered.

Section 2-12 offers a further view of value management and how it can be utilized in the crucial portfolio planning phase.

2.9. Portfolio Management Process Overview

Portfolio management is carried out in an environment broader than the individual portfolio itself, through its roles and processes that relate and cause impact across the whole organization. Portfolio management processes should be within a value-enhancing framework that assists executive management in meeting organizational needs, shareholder and stakeholder expectations, and market or societal needs. As we have discussed, portfolio management links with strategy, operations management, governance, program

Process Groups			
Knowledge Areas	**Defining Process Group**	**Aligning Process Group**	**Authorizing and Controlling Process Group**
Portfolio Strategic Management	Develop portfolio strategic plan. Develop portfolio charter. Define portfolio road map.	Manages strategic change.	
Portfolio Governance Management	Develop portfolio management plan. Define portfolio.	Optimizes portfolio.	Authorizes portfolio. Provides portfolio.
Portfolio Performance Management	Develop portfolio performance. Management plan.	Manages supply and demand. Manages portfolio value.	
Portfolio Communication Management	Develop portfolio communication. Management plan.	Manages portfolio information.	
Portfolio Risk Management	Develop portfolio risk. Management plan.	Manages portfolio risk.	

Table 2-2:   Portfolio management process model (Source: *The Standard for Portfolio Management – Third Edition*, PMI, 2013).

of work, and project management. It enhances transparent and efficient decision making concerning programs of work and supporting activity. The process framework needs to be light and relatively simple in terms of its "fit" with other key process frameworks, especially the finance and strategic planning functions.

Table 2-2 shows a typical high-level model of a portfolio management framework.

2-10. Portfolio Management Process Groups

The following is a series of techniques that we have used many times to assist clients. From those experiences, we have concluded that key functions of portfolio management revolve around the following elements:

- **Enabling** – policy-driven culture of nimbleness and innovation together with controlled risk and opportunity taking.
- **Identifying** – bringing together all sources of input and beginning initial assessment in regard to groupings, coding, and so forth for each portfolio.
- **Balancing** – holistic perspective across opex and capex reviewing value contribution, capacity, priority, capability, risk and opportunity, and selection while aligning with strategic goals and business objectives.
- **Measuring** – performance reviews and analysis at a macro-level to determine trending toward goals and objectives. Use of a light-balanced scorecard is optimal here.
- **Adjusting** – identifying what, how, and when to change portfolio content or other aspects, yet maintaining focus on business objectives and responding quickly to drivers that trigger the need for change.
- **Renewing** – renewing the content of each portfolio as the continuum of investment requires. Typically, this would have a cyclic nature, where portfolio content is adjusted or renewed periodically to maintain rolling-wave designed portfolios.

From these six process elements, we can see how value management provides the overarching guiding mechanism for portfolio management. These elements also allow teams to maintain portfolio focus and differentiate from program of work and project management elements.

Case Study

Recently we had the privilege of working with a particular banking client that allowed us the opportunity to implement a portfolio solution based on a need-to-change initiative. Following the GFC, the bank leaders felt that they needed to look carefully at the overall structure and key functions of its existing program management office. Working closely with their leaders resulted in our client adopting a series of recommendations and other suggestions that transformed the program management office into an enterprise-focused model (EPMO) and, at the same time, connected it to other key functions of strategic planning and finance. Connecting it with those two business units meant that the combined output was coordinated, collated, and collaborated upon. This, together with an investment aimed at maturing their P3M capability, created a great base to launch the beginnings of a portfolio management approach to their overall business model.

Figure 2-3 shows the relationship between portfolio management and the delivery functions of program of work and project management that was deployed via an integrated road map showing the actions required and their interdependencies.

We also developed a library of overarching key functions for each of the portfolio elements.

The client benefits gain was a turnaround from the situation it was in at the beginning of the initiative (i.e., post-GFC vulnerability). Additional benefits were a lift in P3M maturity, a consolidated view of all planned work, and better knowledge that allowed for faster intervention in a troubled program of work and project activity.

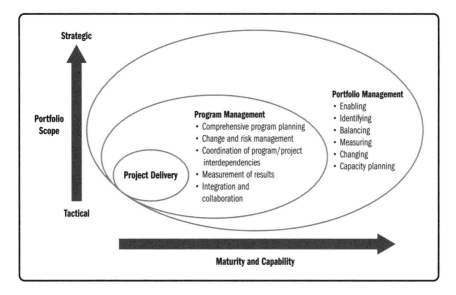

Figure 2-3:   Portfolio management office example.

As an alternative, in the third edition of *The Standard for Portfolio Management,* published by PMI, we see that portfolio processes are typically aggregated into three distinct groups, as follows:

Defining Process Group

This Process Group considers the front-end enablers for effective portfolio management. Using a strategic plan or plans as a starting point, various subplans and other action-oriented outputs are created to form various performance baselines. These drivers would come via other business units, as outlined in Section 2-4. The use of value management techniques as an overarching mechanism would allow for better decision making and better planning outputs to be produced.

Aligning Process Group

This Process Group determines how components will be identified, categorized, evaluated, and selected for inclusion and management of each portfolio.

Authorizing and Controlling Process Group

This Process Group periodically reviews performance indicators for alignment with strategic goals and business objectives. It also provides oversight and communications as well as suggestions regarding changes to any specific group or group of portfolios.

2-11. Portfolio Management Tools and Techniques

What follows is some guidance that will provide a foundation for success in regard to tools and techniques for portfolio management. As a core principle, simplicity needs to be at the forefront. Unfortunately, all too often we see overenthusiastic practitioners being very busy creating a lot of process-oriented material that assists neither the performing group(s) nor the organization. So, from my perspective and experience, I offer the following additional principles:

- Value management is adopted as a model and used as the guiding framework for crafting portfolios.
- Expert judgment is used to support all decision making throughout portfolio development (only if you have the right levels of capability).
- Some form of categorization of portfolio types and components is used.
- Use prioritization models that have weighted criteria for content scoring and selection.
- Use integrated systems for performance reporting that combine data from corporate finance systems, portfolio management systems, and operations systems.
- Use balanced scorecard and other graphical performance reporting systems, such as bubble graphs, trending graphs, and pie charts, to convey key organizational performance data. Section 2-12 offers more on those.

Value Management Framework

This is one area where great improvements can be made in regard to a broader use of portfolio management. It allows the definition and creation of portfolios without becoming handicapped by a detailed process-centric methodology, which seems to be so common. Value management is different from value engineering in that it is a more holistic view toward the creation and sustainability of business value throughout an organization over a longer time period. It is an ideal mechanism to use for strategic implementation management.

We can consider value management as an expanded view of traditional value engineering and of benefits management that links those back to strategic goals and business objectives. It provides a guiding framework that leaders and others can use to form, select, debate, and decide on the content of each of their portfolios. There are five key elements that are required to make up a complete value management model. In summary, these elements are as follows:

- **Value Strategy** – overarching governance and policy that advocates for adoption of value management. Going forward, this guides the strategic conversation around aspects of the business. Examples are value of current relevance, value of change, value of culture, and value of people.
- **Value Planning** – determining and blending opex and capex via the pivot model shown and discussed in Section 2-4.
- **Value Engineering** – optimizing selected and approved options to deliver the best possible value. This can apply to each initiative that has an approved business case, or can be used to enhance a business case for approval.
- **Value Delivery** – implementation excellence via programs of work and project management, to create high fit-for-purpose outputs that lead to outcomes.
- **Value Capturing** – capturing, validating, and confirming value based on, short-, mid- and, where relevant, long-term outcomes associated with each investment. This is a variation on benefits management.

We can group these elements into a P3M viewpoint by considering value strategy and value planning as part of portfolio management. This leads to value engineering and value delivery being

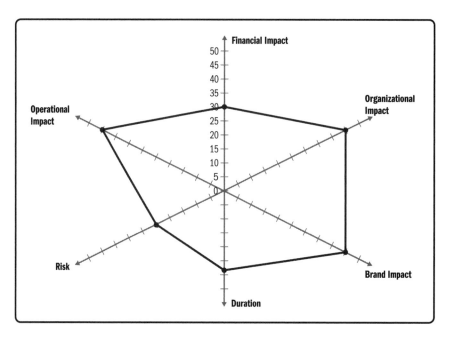

Figure 2-4:   Six-point complexity assessment tool.

considered part of program of work and project management activity. Finally, value capture can be achieved by deploying a form of a benefits management system.

Investment Complexity Assessment

Figure 2-4 shows a six-point assessment tool for assessing the complexity of a proposed investment. By analyzing and scoring each of the six elements, a view of the level of complexity can be gained. This allows good input toward planning, associated with enabling, identifying, balancing, measuring, and changing process elements for each portfolio. The scoring of complexity also provides useful information toward selection and allocation of suitable skill sets as well as an indicator of the likely time periods required for value capture.

Prioritization and Selection Tool Example

Table 2-3 shows an example of a tool that can be utilized to usefully collate various sources of both opex and capex proposed initiatives.

Driver	Max Weight	Initiative A	Initiative B	Initiative C
What is the level of strategic fit?	20	17	14	9
What is the financial value to the organization?	15	12	11	9
What is the immediacy of the need?	15	15	12	8
What is the expected life of the initiative once delivered?	10	9	8	6
How soon will this initiative develop expected benefits?	15	13	10	9
What is the level of complexity?	8	7	7	8
How will this initiative impact our capacity to complete others?	5	4	4	2
What is the level of risk?	12	10	9	8
Totals	**100**	**87**	**75**	**59**

Table 2-3: Example of a prioritization and selection tool.

The example can be adapted to suit your own organization, but I'd suggest that you retain the degree of simplicity that is intended. The use of value management workshops allows robust dialogue around options as well as more informed decisions on investment option taking.

In this example, Initiative A scores higher and would therefore receive a higher portfolio priority than Initiatives B and C.

Tool and Technique Guide

Table 2-4 offers a guide to tools and techniques that can be utilized for each portfolio process group. In all groups, it is critical to remember that expert judgment is applied in addition to data analysis. This is achieved by having a collection of suitable minimum skills available that cover key areas, such as strategic thinking, financial and risk analysis, and portfolio management expertise.

All too often, we see organizations creating a myriad of detailed processes for portfolio management that seem to duplicate existing program of work or project management processes. Having too many processes will tend to choke your organization and stifle its ability to

Table 2-4: Portfolio management tools and techniques with examples.

Process Element	Tools and Techniques Samples	Examples
Enabling	Effective P3M governance. Integrated frameworks. Talent management. Integrated planning. Specific goals and objectives. Portfolio management roles and responsibilities. Appropriate business systems (IT systems). Value strategy.	Steering committees and sponsor. Strong leadership. Enterprise portfolio management office and/or portfolio management office exists. Continuous improvement culture. Increasing P3M maturity. Value management policy guide.
Identifying	Collation of all proposed initiatives. Comparisons of all proposed initiatives. Grouping and categorization of initiatives. Identification of components. Allocation of codes. Value planning.	Component number and description. Strategic objectives supported. Quantitative benefits: new revenues, cost reduction, NPV, ROI, analysis. Value planning.
Balancing	Weighted scoring using enabled criteria. Value planning. Ranking and selection mechanism. Opex versus capex comparisons. Financial modeling. Business case preparation. Business risk versus pure risk. Authorization mechanisms. Value engineering.	Strategic alignment. Productivity and process improvement. Stakeholder satisfaction, competitive advantage. Intellectual property use. Revenue growth. Cost savings or avoidance. Risk: business risk, technology risk, public relations, brand acceptance. Sustainability aspects. Value engineering.
Measuring	P3M software systems. Financial system. Defined P3M frameworks. Performance measuring techniques. Reporting frameworks and tools. Enterprise portfolio management office and/or portfolio management office capability and resources. Value delivery.	Integrated finance and portfolio tools. Integrated and multilevel reporting (e.g., balanced scorecard). Trending analysis and graphical outputs. Comparison analysis against planned benefits. Value analysis. Value capture.
Adjusting	Data analysis and reports. Criteria reweighting. Change management framework. Capacity analysis. Value delivery.	Post-merger and acquisition blending. Market shift or development. Value management analysis. Legislation changes. Value analysis. Value capture.
Renewing	Scenario planning. Performance measurement. Repeat the enabling process group. Value capture.	Continuous improvement culture. Regular planning cycles. Ongoing value management.

respond quickly to a need for change. Because of the longer-term period and rolling-wave nature that portfolios typically have, there is a high probability of change being required. Table 2-4 is very similar to an actual model we developed for a banking client a few years back.

Portfolio Software Tools

Software tools or systems can provide a summary or bird's-eye view of portfolio management activity, allowing the identification of, for example, portfolio problems, program blockages, or project issues. Some software tools allow for the allocation and spreading of resources across portfolios and for keeping a high-level view on each portfolio's progress. Portfolio and program management tools should be integrated, so that supporting infrastructure facilitates seamless communication/exchange between the systems for data collection, tracking and reporting, and so forth to prevent rework and unnecessary duplication.

There are tools available to help organizations realize their further potential by assisting in identifying, selecting, managing, and delivering portfolios that best align with their business strategy. They can help executives gain visibility, insight, and thereby influence and control across their portfolios, programs of work, and projects.

Ideally, these software tools support the entire life cycles associated with programs of work and projects throughout the organization. They follow an initiative from the initial concept through business case analysis, project initiation, various governance phase gates of delivery progress, and final measurement to provide accurate and timely reporting of results, and ultimately, benefits realized and value captured.

By using relevant software tools, multiple levels of organizational benefits can be gained, such as:

- Executive dashboards and other flexible reporting;
- Fully integrated talent/resource management;
- Budgeting, costing, and profitability tracking;
- Intelligent and integrated scheduling, resourcing, and cost management;

- Time and expense tracking, including productive and nonproductive capture;
- Collaboration on document management;
- Integration with other business systems, such as enterprise resource planning (ERP), asset management, and other core tools;
- Embedded frameworks/methodologies and related templates; and
- Customization to suit changing process and future need.

It seems that almost every week, new tools or new versions of existing tools are being released. The marketplace is full of hype around data privacy, cloud computing, software-as-a-service and other offerings, often with a fair degree of rhetoric included. The P3M software arena has not been immune to this hype and that, together with an apparent ongoing confusion of terms used by marketers and salespeople, suggests that caution is required before investing in any software tool solution that is to be used for portfolio management. That said, however, seemingly too many portfolio management office and IT people recommend that low-cost tools, typically used for project planning and control purposes, be purchased/licensed for portfolio management needs. This is a waste of time, money, and energy, which does little to influence the executive leaders that portfolio management, in its true sense, is a viable business model to pursue.

By way of example, there was a telecommunications firm that spent months trying to establish a process-driven software solution from a big-name software company. It turned out that the software did not actually exist! Anecdotal commentary suggests that millions of dollars were spent on consultants and process engineering before a decision was made to terminate the initiative and go back to the perfectly good system the firm already had, but one that was being underutilized because of the capability level of the staff using it and their reluctance to adapt. The firm has since terminated that system and gone in another direction. What this highlights is the lack of detailed consideration of the business needs, the impact of change, and "flavor of the moment" decision making. What is really concerning is that this firm is unlikely to be the only one to have gone through this sequence.

It is, therefore, suggested that organizations take plenty of time to fully define their relevant functional requirements and then conduct relevant research, perhaps using outside assistance, to secure the most up-to-date information prior to making any form of investment in portfolio management software. There is no place for emotion in these important business-critical decisions.

At the risk of incurring wrath and a subsequent war of words, here is a sample of the tools available that may well provide a portfolio management solution for your organizational needs. However, beware of those that use the *project portfolio management* term.

Tools to include in your research should include these samples:

- AMS Realtime Enterprise (www.amsusa.com)
- Artemis Enterprise (www.aisc.com)
- Clarity (www.clarity.com)
- Daptiv PPM for Enterprise PMO (www.daptiv.com)
- Deltek (www.deltek.com)
- Microsoft Project Portfolio Server (www.microsoft.com)
- Oracle Primavera and/or Oracle Insantis (www.oracle .com)
- Planview (www.planview.com)
- Sciforma (www.sciforma.com)

Again, be aware that many P3M software organizations claim to have portfolio management capability in addition to program and project management capability. This is not often the case, because these organizations often confuse the market, and quite possibly themselves, in regard to the use of the term *project portfolio management* instead of just portfolio management.

I should also comment on some enterprise-wide systems, often referred to as enterprise resource planning (ERP) and enterprise asset management (EAM) systems, which can be configured and customized to suit your particular organizational needs. Although these systems are primarily finance oriented, they do offer some form of P3M capability, usually in the form of additional modules.

This capability is more often than not program (read: multiproject) and project oriented, although some offer a claimed "project portfolio management" capability. Though this is encouraging, it seems to me that there is great opportunity for those systems and modules to be developed further to offer a fully integrated portfolio management capability that is beyond many of the current somewhat low-level offerings available currently.

Therefore, many executives, including CIOs, get confused and then possibly end up agreeing to the purchase of a P3M system as a result of bad advice or the "flavor of the moment" syndrome.

A critical decision like this requires balanced and independent input from an expert who understands the organization's level of P3M maturity, the type of work done, the mix of opex and capex expenditure, and the complexity across the organization, both now and into the midterm.

2-12. Portfolio Management Metrics and Reporting

Portfolio metrics are typically fashioned from aggregated measures of key information from a variety of sources. Ideally, those should be shown in a balanced scorecard format. We have all seen organizations producing reports that have far too much information and provide little assistance to the report's recipients. Again, the secret to success is to be simple in design yet powerful in terms of content and shared understanding. A well-designed dashboard and/or report should offer data and executive commentary on some or all of these factors:

- Strategic goal and/or business objective progress, with each separated and clearly labeled;
- Financial status and time to value together with projected savings and non-drawdown of reserves;
- Split of opex and capex status in a rolled-up consolidation;
- Risk profile, including consolidated view; and
- Consolidated portfolio data.

Portfolio Management Reporting

Reporting on the progression of various portfolios needs to be high level and aligned to the organization's strategy and related objectives. Ideally, the content, performance, and balancing are all tightly linked to other organizational reporting. Some examples of report types and content are:

- Balanced scorecard across all portfolios;
- Portfolio performance metrics;
- Program of work reporting:
  - Benefit achievement;
  - Asset maintenance and development status;
  - Risk profile; and
  - Resource capability;
- Project reporting in a summarized manner, if not part of a program of work; and
- Financial reporting:
  - Key indicators that determine balance and content of each portfolio;
  - Consolidated views on forecast end costs of each portfolio, including savings and non-drawdown of reserves; and
  - Benefits realization—actual and projected.

In general terms, it is best to have an integrated reporting model that focuses on the portfolio level and caters to an executive audience. Other forms of reporting, such as program of work and project reporting, can be developed and distributed at lower levels of the organization.

Figure 2-5 indicates an integrated solution model on reporting, which should minimize duplication, streamline data, and reduce production time.

Executive reporting at the portfolio level needs to offer information on the critical aspects or critical success factors (CSFs) of the organization's business. Information needs to be collated in different ways, so that each reader group is provided with

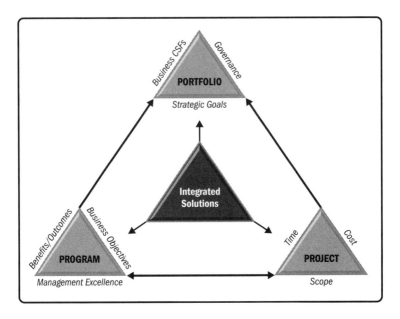

Figure 2-5: Integrated solutions model.

information that is relevant and pertinent to their level of decision making and stakeholder interest. Be warned that rolled-up project management data, though vital for program of work reporting, are not sufficient for portfolio reporting.

For portfolio reporting, a balanced scorecard (BSC) approach is best. However, this needs to be a light version, not a full-blown theoretical model that will choke the organization with its unwieldiness and time and cost to deliver.

The balanced scorecard was developed by Dr. Robert Kaplan and Dr. David Norton of the Harvard Business School as a performance measurement framework, which added strategic non-financial performance measures to traditional financial metrics to provide leaders with a more "balanced" view of organizational performance. This is seen as a strategic planning and management system, not just a measurement system, that helps organizations translate strategy into operational themes, which then drive behavior, and ultimately, higher performance.

The adoption of the BSC has often been criticized as being too cumbersome and not appropriate for smaller organizations. The economic turmoil of the past few years has reminded leaders that greater organizational performance is required. However, this performance is more than just bottom-line financial tracking. Instead, it is a more mature and balanced consideration of other elements important to today's need for a more dynamic organization. Some of our clients' comments indicate that there is a growing movement toward more sophisticated systems that provide more alignment and connection with strategy and operational plans. This is supported by the increasing adoption of portfolio and program management approaches to "getting stuff done." It's now time to reconsider the BSC in a more flexible manner, which has fewer objectives, targets, and measures to give a light version. From a change management perspective, a light version is more likely to successfully gain stakeholder buy-in, and therefore be sustainable, leading to higher and longer-lasting organizational performance.

My opinion is that too many organizations use a dashboard of consolidated project data together with detailed financial information to report portfolio and/or program of work performance as a BSC substitute. This provides only a two-dimensional and somewhat limited view and, therefore, an unbalanced perspective. Executives should demand additional information that is balanced (four-dimensional, as per Figure 2-6) for improved governance and better-informed decision making, while continually assessing corporate risk.

The close compatibility between BSC and portfolio management lends itself well to organizations that are seeking more mature contributions from their existing EPMO or portfolio management offices. These can provide a valuable contribution by working closely with finance, strategy planning, and others as required to provide a central collation and analysis service to the entire organization. Ownership of the BSC can be within the EPMO, but only if its leadership and staff have the maturity, capability, and vision required to operate effectively at a portfolio level that is focused at the enterprise level.

In summary, the BSC takes four perspectives or themes and breaks them down, in much the same way as a work breakdown structure does with scope, to determine objectives, measures, and targets. From this comes a series of initiatives (projects) that together provide the linkages and thereby break down the barriers. In my view, the organizational objectives can be viewed as programs of work, the measures and targets as benefits, and the initiatives as projects. Overall, a BSC can be seen as a single organizational portfolio of work, or perhaps a group of portfolios (i.e., a portfolio for each strategic theme). However, it needs to be light.

The BSC can be supplemented by the inclusion of bubble chart, pie chart, and histogram-type infographics, supplemented by trending information on CSFs. The result is a content-rich and highly intuitive report, which is easy to understand yet conveys specific key information that revolves around the critical success factors of the organization.

Figure 2-6 shows an example of a BSC report model.

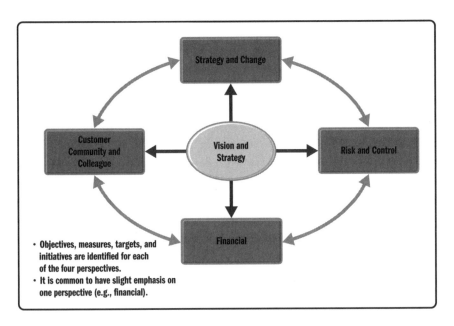

Figure 2-6: Balanced scorecard model.

	Project	Program of Work	Portfolio	Business
Strategic Line of Sight	Project Metrics (maximum 20)	Performance Dashboard Indicators (approx. 12)	Trend-Based Indicators (approx. 8)	Critical Success Factors (CSFs) (6 Strategy Goals)
Audience	Project Managers	Program of Work Managers	Portfolio Managers and General Managers (VPs)	Executive and Board
Report Type	Project Status	Program Dashboard	Portfolio Performance	Balanced Scorecard
P3M Tool	Project Management Tool	Program Management Tool	Enterprise Portfolio System	ERP System
People and Systems	Project Input and Output	Roll-Up and Outcomes	Trending Toward Goals and Objectives	Value Affirmation

Table 2-5:   Integrated reporting example.

Case Study

Table 2-5 shows an actual example of an integrated portfolio, program of work, and project management reporting model for a telecommunications client. We had been asked to analyze and design an integrated solution that provided different levels of information drawn from a common data source. Once developed, it filled a large gap of key data that the CEO and his leadership team had identified—that is, in terms of status trending toward critical success factors, which they had established from the organization's strategy plan.

The model was designed, built, tested, then implemented. After some fine-tuning, it provided the level of data and insight that the CEO and his team required. It provided a good route toward integrated reporting across the whole organization. It was relatively simple and it worked.

There is a great temptation in status reporting to create complex report structures that contain far too much information for the intended audience. Common mistakes include people packing information into it that aims to suit all audiences—a one-size-fits-all approach. We are constantly reminded that busy executives and those in governance roles have limited time. Whether limitation of time is good or bad is best discussed elsewhere. However, we do need to cater to this by producing report outputs that are succinct, focused on the needs of the reader group, and most important, invite dialogue and questions among leaders and others.

For more on specific program of work and project reporting, see Section 3–9, which offers insights and commentary on reporting approaches and formats, with further examples for each.

S E C T I O N

Using Program and Project Management to Deliver Change and Realize Benefits

3-1. Program Management Explained

Put simply, programs of work are a breakdown of content from authorized portfolios. They establish planned and authorized packages of work that are required to be executed within an agreed-upon time frame, budget, scope, and so on. The use of programs of work makes good business and logical sense, as it allows packages of work to be considered, grouped, planned, and executed in a holistic, coordinated, and efficient manner. This applies equally to opex- and capex-related work. An example of an opex application is an electricity company grouping planned maintenance replacements of assets or even parts of assets into a program of work. This provides benefits via economy-of-scale purchasing and also productivity through more efficient production work. That program of work can be part of a portfolio that focuses on asset enhancement or maintenance. A capex example of a program of work within an electricity company is an integrated group of generation, transmission, and distribution initiatives, which deliver a new or increased capability and capacity to the performing organization. Business benefit is gained through greater amounts of electricity being sold to customers, which includes revenue gain, increased customer market share, and likely increased brand profile.

The use of project management techniques should be quite well known to readers of this book. However, it is worth highlighting that future use of project management needs to consider more than just a delivery focus. The almost hardwired connection with program management suggests that project management practitioners could influence program of work and, perhaps, portfolio managers much more in terms of program of work definition and component makeup.

The following definitions are provided for clarity:

Program:

> A group of related projects, subprograms, and program activities that are managed in a coordinated way to obtain benefits not available from managing them individually. (PMI, 2013c, pp. 4, 116)

Program of Work:
Programs of work include elements of related work outside the scope of the discrete projects that are grouped into the program of work. An example is opex-related work that is grouped and included in some manner for efficiency gains.

Program Management:

> The application of knowledge, skills, tools, and techniques to a program to meet the program requirements and to obtain benefits and control not available by managing projects individually. (PMI, 2013c, pp. 6, 167)

Program of Work Management:

Program of work management is similar to program management but includes those management activities associated with operational expenditure.

3-2. A Program Life Cycle

Good practice is to break a program of work into discrete phases or stages. These are often sequential phases, or perhaps subprojects, that have interdependencies. The phases facilitate program governance, enhanced control and coordination of program and project resources, and overall risk management, together with any opportunity enhancement. The focus of program of work management is on outcomes and downstream benefits, whereas a project life cycle focuses on producing outputs or deliverables.

The type of program of work being managed may influence the life cycle; however, the major life cycle phases and their deliverables will remain similar. Figure 3-1 shows a typical program of work life cycle.

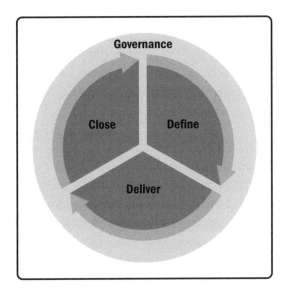

Figure 3-1:   A typical program of work life cycle.

The deliver phase is where the major effort and time are expended. Benefits are often progressively gained over a defined period.

Senior management, via steering committees, needs to be involved with governance reviews, usually at phase-gate points, to ensure that each program of work delivers the expected outcomes, that expected benefits are still relevant to the approved business case, and the program of work complies with organizational governance requirements.

3-3. Differences Between Program and Project Life Cycles

Although program of work and project life cycles are similar in nature, because of the need to define content, budget, plan, and schedule, and manage aspects of risk, change, and other elements relating to stakeholder expectations, some key differences include the following:

- Programs of work often have an extended life cycle and duration, as some projects transition to operations when other projects are just commencing.
- Programs of work often deliver outcomes, as they collate outputs from component projects and other work. Those outcomes are usually expressed as benefits.
- Outputs, or capabilities, delivered by individual projects within the program of work are usually integrated in order to provide some or all of the expected benefits from the program of work.
- Projects facilitate, and become the catalyst for, discrete benefits at the end of their life cycle, and those benefits subsequently contribute toward the overall program of work benefits.
- Within a program of work, initiatives may use different life cycle models or approaches depending on the actual work content.

3-4. Program Management Performance Domains

Five domains permeate all activities within a program of work. The domains are:

- Program Strategic Alignment
- Program Governance
- Program Benefits Management
- Program Stakeholder Management
- Program Life Cycle Management

Those domains evolve over the duration of the program of work and require both the program sponsors' and the program managers' focus throughout each phase of the program life cycle. Some further details on each domain follow.

Domain 1 – Program Strategy Alignment

The degree of alignment practiced will depend on the P3M maturity of the performing organization, and whether or not portfolio management is utilized throughout the organization. If the organization utilizes portfolio management in collaboration with value management, then most of the strategy alignment will have been done during the portfolio planning period. In this situation, the focus needs to be on work authorization (i.e., each program of work that is part of a portfolio needs to be authorized via a specific business case). The production and approval of each business case will also determine the order and timing of commencement of each program of work.

If portfolio management is not utilized in the organization, then this domain step becomes very important, as it allows for analysis and consideration of each proposed program of work to be done in the context of the organization's strategic objectives, which are reflected in its annual plan. This is an important step and is therefore usually done by senior managers or executives who act, sometimes without knowing it, in a program governance role. Like any form of consideration, this group will consider investment case and monetary input required, risks, expected outcomes, and value to the organization by way of returns. They will want to satisfy themselves that the value that is being sought contributes clearly to one or more business objectives.

Domain 2 – Program Governance

As discussed in Section 1-5 (refer back to Figure 1-8), organizational P3M governance includes the domains of portfolio, program, and project management. Therefore, program governance needs to fit within the wider governance of the organization.

Program governance is an accountability framework for efficient and effective decision making and delivery management. It is concerned with controlling the investment and monitoring delivery of benefits. It is the process of developing, communicating, implementing, monitoring, and assuring the policies, procedures, organizational structures, and practices associated with each program of work are followed.

This is achieved via regular progress reviews and reports and specifically at the end of each program of work life cycle phase. These phase gates allow accountable senior management to assess performance before authorizing the program of work to move to the next phase.

Program governance also monitors the progress of the program via the coordinated delivery of the outputs from its component projects.

Program Steering Committee

A program steering committee, sometimes referred to as a governance board, is a key forum, whereby blockages and issues affecting the program of work can be discussed and resolved. The steering committee, chaired by the program of work sponsor, represents the interests of the organization and provides overarching program governance, including quality assurance, to the program of work and its leader. Ideally, the program steering committee should be an appropriately sized, cross-functional subset of executive managers who are responsible for providing guidance and decisions regarding direction and changes affecting program of work outcomes.

Typical functions of the program steering committee include, but are not limited to:

- Initiation of each program of work;
- Approval of program plans and authorization of any major deviations;
- Overview of progress, benefits delivery, and costs;
- Guidance on issues;
- Assurance of resource availability;
- Collection of input for strategic progress reporting;
- Establishment of frameworks and limits for making decisions about ongoing investments in the program of work; and
- Compliance with corporate and legal policies, procedures, standards, and requirements.

A program steering committee should *not* be a consensus committee; the executive sponsor needs to be *the* key decision maker, taking input, advice, and commitments from others within the steering committee and the program of work leader as required. The committee members do not work full-time on the program; therefore, they should empower the program management team and thereby rely on them.

Governance activities are conducted through each phase of the program of work life cycle. Phase-gate reviews provide an opportunity for steering committee members to:

- Ensure that the program of work remains viable and continues to support the organization's strategic plan via the expected benefits being sought,
- Review and resolve critical program risks and issues, and
- Approve program continuation or cancel (terminate) the program if the situation warrants.

Domain 3 – Program Benefits Management

Benefits management, also referred to as benefits realization, is the definition and formalization of the expected benefits a program of work is intended to deliver by way of outcomes. This can include both tangible and intangible benefits and the planning, modeling, and tracking of intermediate and final results throughout the program life cycle. The most commonly sought-after benefits are of a tangible nature. Tangible benefits are quantifiable, and therefore, measurable, and may relate to specific business performance aspects. Examples in a for-profit environment are revenue, cost savings, market share growth, and product sales volume. A nonprofit organization may gain benefits by reducing effort time or cost, thereby gaining benefits by becoming more efficient.

Intangible benefits, such as improved employee morale or brand profile, are less easily quantified because of their subjective nature. This leads to doubt and debate on the reality of actual outcomes. Those who are new to benefits realization should ignore them and base proposed business cases on tangible benefits only. This drives focus throughout the program of work period and especially post-program output, that is, during the benefit (value capture) period. The real gain to an organization is the clarity on just what benefit (value) has been gained toward and following completion of the program of work.

Benefits Management Throughout the Life Cycle

The program of work life cycle should be designed to comply with the needs of corporate governance and organizational processes. However, it should also be designed to ensure that the expected benefits are realized in a predictable and coordinated manner. Benefits management has a life cycle that runs parallel to that of the program of work, and it evolves as the program of work scope evolves. Benefits management begins in the initiation phases of a program life cycle when the proposed program of work is articulated as a business case. This assists the organization to realize and sustain the stated benefits from the investment, as most of those will often materialize after the conclusion of the program of work life cycle. Figure 3-2 shows how

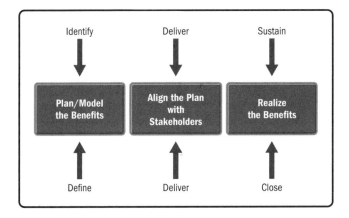

Figure 3-2: Benefits management and the program of work life cycle.

benefits management and a program of work life cycle relate to each other.

There should be clear definition and agreement among decision makers on the factors contributing to benefits, as well as a supporting structure and processes to help plan, manage, measure, track, and realize the benefits. The benefits expected from each project investment within the program of work should be defined in the business case before the program of work is initiated, together with an overview of the tracking and assessment processes. It is recommended that, initially, only tangible benefits be considered, until such time as the overall maturity of the organization reaches a higher level.

Each program of work phase should be capable of recording, tracking, and evaluating benefits in accordance with the approved business case, or a reassessed situation if performance was negatively affected in a previous phase. A benefits management plan (BMP) should be prepared, which summarizes all aspects of identifying, delivering, and sustaining benefits associated with each program of work.

Periodic benefits realization reviews need to be conducted, often at phase-gate reviews, where reporting shows planned versus actual benefits, as well as forecasting their ongoing value, reasons for any deviations, and recommendations on how they can be adjusted.

Domain 4 – Program Stakeholder Management

Stakeholders are individuals and organizations whose interests may be affected by the outcome of a program of work, either positively or negatively. Stakeholders can be both internal and external to the organization, and be at any level of an organization's hierarchy.

Key stakeholders often play a critical role in the success of a program of work or project, so one must consider their interests and concerns.

Both program of work and project management teams must identify stakeholders early in their respective life cycles and actively manage stakeholder expectations throughout all stages to ensure their continued support of the program and its components.

Significant changes in the program of work or project environment may add or remove stakeholders; the program of work or project manager must take appropriate and proactive actions to manage expected and actual changes.

The engagement of many stakeholders can provide valuable input. They have the ability to influence programs of work, and they can help or hinder, depending on the benefits or threats (sometimes referred to as *dis-benefits*) they see.

Program of work and project managers must understand the position stakeholders have taken (or may take), the way they may exert their influence, and their source of power (i.e., their ability and ease of influence).

Stakeholders may be groups of individuals who are competing for your resources or are pursuing objectives that conflict with those of your program of work. Individual stakeholders may not be directly affected by the results of the program of work, but maintain an interest in the initiative.

A stakeholder management plan that is related and blended with a communications plan are proven tools for delivering accurate, consistent, and timely information to stakeholder groups. This is to facilitate a clear understanding of program of work and project objectives and their current issues.

Program of work stakeholder management is wider than project stakeholder management, as it considers additional levels of stakeholders resulting from broader interdependencies across, and often outside, the organization. The associated stakeholder and communication plan needs to be proactive, targeted, and integrated. It should be structured in a manner that seeks to deliver key messages and develop engagement with stakeholders at the right time and in the right manner.

Approach to Stakeholder Management

No matter how large or small your program of work initiative is, its success is dependent on how well you identify and subsequently manage stakeholder expectations. With increasing levels of complexity across many programs of work and a delivery success rate that seems constantly under pressure, it is now critical that this important area, which combines stakeholder management and their communications needs, remains high on the priority list of tasks for each program of work manager.

However, stakeholder management does not need to be overly complicated. There is a natural link between stakeholder management and communications management. Therefore, in most situations, the amount of time spent on this by the program of work manager should be considerable.

Figure 3-3 shows a typical and relatively simple four-step process-cycle approach to stakeholder management. The steps allow you to:

- Identify stakeholders who may be affected by the program of work. Once identified, they should be grouped, for example, using an affinity diagram or something similar, in some manner that allows for easier downstream analysis;
- Analyze each group to consider level of influence as well as level of impact. This includes specific individuals as necessary (you may wish to consider their levels of power and importance should you that consider relevant);
- Develop an engagement and communication strategy and build a plan to engage the stakeholders, either individually or in groups;

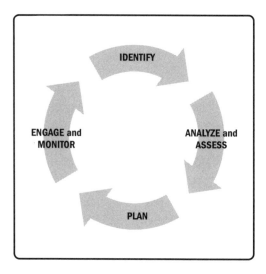

Figure 3-3: Typical approach to stakeholder management.

- Engage and manage their expectations while seeking to increase their level of support;
- Apply ongoing management via communications, and seek to improve their acceptance of the objectives and benefits of each program of work; and
- Repeat the process as often as necessary.

Stakeholder Analysis

Figure 3-4 provides a matrix in which stakeholders can be analyzed according to their relative influence and impact (sometimes referred to as importance and power). Thus, the level of stakeholder management and communication can be assessed. Program of work managers and others involved need to understand the position stakeholders may take, the way they may exert their influence, and the impacts of each. To assist with this, a continuum of engagement can be used to guide the level and type of engagement. For example, you will need to get strong buy-in from those stakeholders that map onto the "crucial" area of the simple matrix, whereas you will only need to periodically inform those in the "minimal" area. Where

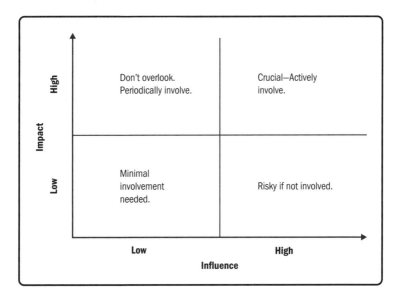

Figure 3-4: Stakeholder analysis and management matrix.

negative influence is identified, one needs to ensure that these stakeholders can see the benefits to them, as well as to the organization.

Influence refers to how powerful a stakeholder is, whereas importance refers to the degree to which consideration of a stakeholder's problems, needs, and interests must be prioritized to ensure success of the initiative. Influence is the power that stakeholders can exert on a program of work, or on an individual component of that program of work, to affect the decisions made when it suits their need. This power can be a positive or negative impact.

Using simple and proven tools, such as a stakeholder register, categorization tool, engagement log, and a matrix tool that uses a form of RACI (responsible, accountable, consulted, informed) approach, provide a solid platform for success in stakeholder and communications management. Programs of work often have significant elements of change inherent within them. Therefore, the program of work manager needs to be prepared to spend a considerable amount of time on stakeholder and communications management throughout the whole of the program of work life cycle.

Domain 5 – Program Life Cycle Management

This is where program of work managers will spend most of their effort, guiding and supporting project teams, while also keeping a close eye on the larger aspects of the program of work. As in the previous domain areas, a strong stakeholder and communications focus is necessary to successfully complete a program of work. Furthermore, program of work managers must constantly consider and assess the state of the program in terms of change effectiveness and capturing planned benefits. To do this, they will apply management skills across additional supporting areas, such as financial, integration, procurement, quality, resource, risk, schedule, and program scope. Multiple levels of change management will need to be applied (e.g., changes to any of the supporting areas and changes to the organization itself, which is the catalyst for benefits to be captured).

3-5. Program of Work Breakdown

All programs of work should be broken down into phases for better planning, control, and governance purposes. Circumstances such as scale, complexity, and volume of programs will influence how the breakdown is applied. As guidance, here is a five-phase breakdown guide to consider.

Phase 1 – Program of Work Initiation

The primary objective of this phase is to establish a firm foundation of support and approval for the program of work. This is usually via an approved business case. The activity leading to an approved business case would typically involve:

- Understanding the strategic value of the proposed initiative;
- Identifying the key decision makers/stakeholders and their expectations and interests;
- Defining program of work objectives and their alignment with the organization's strategic objectives or approved portfolio;

- Developing a high-level business case demonstrating an understanding of the needs, alignment to a portfolio, feasibility, justification, and expected benefits;
- Securing approval for the program of work from the steering committee;
- Appointing the program of work manager; and
- Developing a plan to initiate the program of work via a program charter or something similar.

A program charter would include high-level scope, objectives, budget, and time frame. More information and data would show how the program of work maps to business objectives and what benefits are envisioned.

Phase 2 – Program Setup

Based on the program of work life cycle shown in Figure 3-1, the program of work has now passed the first governance gate and has received some form of approval to proceed, possibly an approved business case from a steering committee. Setting up should initially focus on building a detailed road map with clear direction and definition of key components and changes. Then, generate a detailed program management plan that evolves from the road map and includes program makeup in terms of what project outputs are to be produced and the anticipated downstream benefits. Information on when, whom, how much it will cost, risks and issues, program interdependencies, assumptions, constraints, and how the program of work will be managed during its execution period would typically also be included. The program management plan will include various subplans as necessary.

Somewhat in parallel to the development of the program management plan would be the initial creation of a benefits management plan. The benefits management plan would attempt to show the short-, mid-, and longer-term benefits to be realized following delivery of each component project's deliverables/outputs. Depending on how the organization is structured, the benefits plan could be developed by persons/groups other than the program of work manager, for example, as a function done by a program management office.

Phase 3 – Establish Program Delivery Infrastructure

This infrastructure will support the program of work and component projects as they begin to deliver the outputs and initial benefits of the program. At this point, the program of work has passed the second phase gate, so the program manager has the mandate to execute the next phase, as defined by its program management plan. The supporting infrastructure that each program of work often requires includes:

- Defined and often specific governance structures with corresponding processes and procedures;
- Various organizational tools, such as enterprise resource planning (ERP), program and project management tools, benefits measurement, and so on;
- Program office capabilities that provide mentoring, coaching, professional development, and other facilities; and
- Access to ample quantities of the skilled resources required for key program of work and component project teams.

Each program of work that is being implemented requires a program organization structure to support the control and monitoring of the program of work and its projects by making decisions for the program of work at a tactical level. This specific structure may consist of:

- Steering Committee – accountable and responsible for complete program of work governance;
- Program of Work Sponsor – usually an executive who is primarily accountable to the business for delivery of benefits. He or she should chair the steering committee;
- Program Director/Manager – responsible for managing, representing, and delivering the program of work in its entirety;
- Program Team – responsible for delivery of the program management plan or components of the program, either singularly or collectively; and

- Program Management Office – supports the program manager and the program team as well as the organization in terms of validation of benefits over the benefits realization period.

There is also a strong change management element to this phase as the program of work transitions from the current state toward the desired future state. Change management techniques need to be applied in parallel with this phase of the program of work and during the delivery activity.

Phase 4 – Initial Benefits Delivery

The purpose of this phase is to conclude the delivery of the component project outputs to at least commencement of the initial incremental benefits. At this point, the program of work has passed the third phase gate, and the core work of the program, through its components, physically begins. This phase needs to be controlled well, as some activities are repeated as often as required, and the benefits begin to be achieved in a cumulative manner. The phase ends when the planned benefits of the program have been captured, or a governance decision to terminate the program of work has been made. Examples of specific activities conducted during this phase include:

- Initiating, controlling, and concluding component projects;
- Managing, via change management, transition from current state to future state;
- Ensuring adherence to program and project management frameworks, methodologies, processes, and so forth;
- Ensuring that individual component projects meet all requirements;
- Identifying environmental changes and related stakeholder interests;
- Coordinating common activities or dependencies across the program of work;
- Ensuring that risks, issues, and changes are well managed;

- Coordinating the efficient use of resources across the program of work; and
- Communicating with stakeholders and the program board.

Within a program of work, some projects may produce benefits that are realized immediately, whereas other projects may deliver output capability that must be integrated with outputs capabilities delivered by other projects before the associated benefits can be realized.

Realization of the final benefits identified in the approved business case usually happens at some point after the final output/deliverable from each component project has been delivered. It is this aspect that suggests that program and project managers should not be accountable for the realization of the intended benefits. The accountability must be with the person or group that has greater oversight of activity within the organization. This accountability should be with the program of work sponsor of each program of work. The sponsor may consider the delegation of this accountability to an enterprise portfolio management office or program of work management office to be beneficial, thus by giving it day-to-day responsibility for monitoring and reporting the capture of benefits over a stated period. So, though it is reasonable that the responsibility can be delegated to others as appropriate, the accountability for the ultimate success of the program of work remains with the program sponsor.

Phase 5 – Close the Program

Here, the program of work has passed the fourth and final phase gate, where all component work is physically complete and benefits are accruing. This phase sees a controlled close down of the program of work, the decommissioning of the program's organizational structure, transition of artifacts, ongoing benefits monitoring, and transition to operational or other groups. Key activities to ensure smooth and issue-free program closure should include the following:

- Review the status of the program of work, its change, and the status of benefits with the program sponsor.

- Disband the program organization, program team, and any remaining project team members.
- Dismantle infrastructure and reconcile as necessary.
- Document lessons learned and provide feedback to the program sponsor, EPMO, and others as appropriate.
- Store key documents and other artifacts.

3-6. Capturing Value (Benefits Realization)

Programs of work have an inherent change element within them. This change is simply the difference between the current state and the desired future state. The desired future state should align to at least one objective from the organization's business plan. The change results in desired outcome (i.e., the situation that occurs as a result of the changes made). Benefits are the quantification of these outcomes and are used to direct the program of work, inform decision making along the way, and validate achievement against business objectives. Change may also result in unintended consequences, which sometime lead to *dis-benefits* (i.e., benefits that have a negative impact on the desired outcome or on stakeholders). Unintended consequences and other side effects can sometimes lead to additional, likely unplanned, benefits.

The identification, planning, monitoring, and measurement of benefits are fundamental parts of successful program of work management.

The use of a value management framework will greatly enhance the quality of envisioned benefits that are subsequently captured, as they will have been carefully considered from an early perspective in the value planning and value engineering workshops.

Benefits may be identified from many different sources and can be grouped accordingly, such as by classification, category, business impact, value type, and change type. There is a need to be consistent here, so limit this to the use of only a small number of groupings. This will be beneficial in the short and medium terms, as it will allow for consistent understanding and thereby be used throughout the organization. If we refer back to the global situations that were discussed in Section 1, then "business impact" and "change type" should be used as initial groupings. In *Benefits Realisation Management* (2006), Gerald Bradley offered the business impact group headings of "strategic," "speculative," "key operational," and "support." In the support the model offered in Figure 1-1, Bradley's strategic and speculative categories fit well in the "getting ahead" continuum, and his key operational and support categories clearly reside in the "staying in business" side of the continuum. The use of "change type" as a grouping also sits well in today's fast-changing environment, as it offers group titles of "doing new things," "doing existing things better," and "stopping the doing of existing things."

Whichever benefits groupings you select, there are some key points to remember as you develop your benefit realization processes:

- Maintain executive support and ownership.
- Keep your process simple.
- Use only tangible benefits initially. (All benefits should be quantified numerically.)
- Make sure that accountability and responsibility are well defined.
- Consider a focus on short- to midterm benefits that relate to business plan objectives.

The adoption of a value management framework and a realistic approach to benefits management will allow your organization to mature toward becoming a higher-performing entity. Your organization should capture success that has been driven through a mind-set that has embraced the 3 Ps to Success (purpose, people, performance) mentioned in Section 1-7, so that aligned activity, empowered people, growth, efficiency, and brand enhancement are the results.

3-7. Program Management Process Groups

Program management process groups are quite similar to those process groups found in a project management environment. It is quite common that these process groups overlap, somewhat depending on circumstances and the context of each program of work.

However, key differences are that process groups deployed at a program of work level generally focus at a higher level, whereas a project will focus more on the detailed content of the project scope and its associated process groups. Some context examples are component interdependencies, change management, benefits, and overall program of work risk. It should be highlighted that stakeholder management is now generally seen as a specific performance domain of program of work management. Thus, it is generally not included as a supporting or lower-level process group of program management. Other, albeit lesser, differences are that cost management is defined as financial management at the program of work level and that HR management is defined as resource management. Other supporting process groups such as scope, risk, schedule, quality, communications, risk, and integration are common to both program of work and project levels.

As mentioned in the paragraph above, context and circumstances will guide the program of work leader on just how these process groups are deployed in your organization. However, some common inputs and outputs would include assumptions, constraints, historical information, organization process assets (e.g., policies, procedures, processes, guidelines), and enterprise environmental factors (e.g., market, economy, regulatory, technology, etc.).

3-8. Program Management Tools and Techniques

Some of the tools and techniques used in portfolio management can be adapted for use in a program management environment. However, the tools and techniques commonly utilized in a program management environment are more similar to those used in a project management environment. One key difference, however, is that a benefits realization period can be incorporated into the overall program of work business case and subsequent plan.

There is no substitute for planning. Whether it's at the organizational level, program of work level, or at the project level, planning is the key to overcoming complex and complicated challenges. People who seek a "quick fix" or easy solution and expect sustained organizational performance improvements are delusional. Current failure rates of projects attest to that.

Typical techniques used for program management should include the following:

People: Recognize that program of work management requires a higher skill set and experience level than project management. Invest in your people's capabilities to match your business plan and portfolio demands.

Expert Judgment: Use subject matter experts (SMEs) obtained from internal and external sources. This is used to break down portfolio grouping into various programs of work and individual projects.

Meetings: Apply a transparent and nonbiased approach to facilitation, deliberation, and decision making. Participants must have the authority to make decisions regarding program of work matters.

P3M Governance: Require management or peer reviews on business case approvals, status, plans, phase-gate reviews/approvals, benefit reviews, and so forth. Combine with SMEs as necessary.

Policies and Procedures: Develop these to implement standards, processes, and work methods in a consistent manner. They can include classification of information, restrictions on distribution, requirements for retention, specific contents for artifacts (e.g., program management plan), framework/methodology to be used, governance process, and risk management. Some form of PMO should ideally be in place to facilitate policies and procedures on behalf of all program of work teams within the organization.

In regard to software tools that can be used, the sample software tools list provided in Section 2-11 also apply here. That said, there are many more software tool offerings at the program level, as desktop tools can be included as options. There is an increasing number of program and project manager productivity tools available on the market, with many offered as SaaS (software-as-a-service) via cloud or externally hosted means. Software tools that have benefits management capability are beginning to make an appearance; however, this is still a relatively new area of functionality for many software providers. As stated in Section 2, and worth repeating here, care is needed to make sure that organizational needs, including supply chain needs, are carefully analyzed prior to investing in any software tools that are to be used for the management and control of programs of work.

3-9. Program Management Metrics and Reporting

The key to success here is to recognize that program of work reporting typically sits at a higher level than individual project reporting, but typically lower than that used for portfolio management. The introduction of benefits reporting, if benefits management is being applied, is the key difference from project reporting.

Program management controls are required to be applied to all program of work activity. These are similar in context to classic project controls, but may vary as a result of specific circumstances. Examples include standards, frameworks, reporting, contracts, regulations, policies, and procedures. Typically, the metrics reported against are at the program of work level and therefore need to embrace and comment on higher-level aspects of each program of work, such as overall progress, overall risks, overall financial status, benefits planned versus benefits realized, change, and stakeholder matters.

The overarching mantra of reporting program of work status is "striving for simplicity." In other words, it is better to have a one-page report for each program of work that has a high probability of being read than having numerous pages of detailed report for each program of work that is unlikely to be read, critiqued, or even understood.

Case Study

This is an example from a power distribution company that we were assisting. Each month, a small program management office team collated and produced all its capex project data into two reports using the same report format. One report showed individual project status, while the other showed a rolled-up program of work status that summarized all capex projects. Those reports were distributed to various business group leaders and other key stakeholders as necessary. Each program of work had produced a one-page report, which was analyzed and collated further to reveal the complete status of all work, timings, risks, actual costs, savings, and reserves.

Furthermore, our team produced an executive/board level report for the CEO and board of directors, summarizing all capex and opex performance that showed the complete financial picture of the company at that point in time into a single report format that was highly graphical and supported with summary narratives. This report summarized key financial information and risk that directly compared to the approved annual business plan. Like the program of work format, this report also revealed the complete status of all work, timings and cash flows, risks, cost savings, and reserves status.

Figure 3-5 shows the one-page format used for reporting on a program of work. You can note the emphasis on business-like metrics of cost, time, risk, and the summary style. If required, this one-page format can be supplemented with other relevant and supporting material, such as infographics on cost, benefits highlights, and so on.

3-10. Project Management Commentary

This section provides an overview of project management as it is applicable today, and the challenges that need to be overcome for project management to be an effective delivery vehicle for portfolio and program of work management.

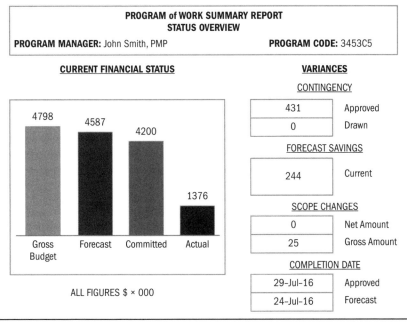

PROGRAM of WORK SUMMARY REPORT
STATUS OVERVIEW

PROGRAM MANAGER: John Smith, PMP   **PROGRAM CODE:** 3453C5

CURRENT FINANCIAL STATUS

4798	4587	4200		
Gross Budget	Forecast	Committed	1376 Actual	

ALL FIGURES $ × 000

VARIANCES

CONTINGENCY

431	Approved
0	Drawn

FORECAST SAVINGS

244	Current

SCOPE CHANGES

0	Net Amount
25	Gross Amount

COMPLETION DATE

29-Jul-16	Approved
24-Jul-16	Forecast

1. **Executive Overview:**

1.1 This program of work consisting of six projects replaces the existing outdoor substation with a new and bigger substation on client land directly adjacent to the existing substation site. The existing outdoor switchgear and substation is to be dismantled via a separate project after the commissioning of the new substation.

2. **Scope:**

2.1 No scope changes authorized to date. Benefits capture on track.

3. **Schedule:**

3.1 The three-week slippage identified previously has been recovered, and the commissioning date is now shown as five (5) days early.

4. **Financial:**

4.1 Major commitments yet to be made are the landscaping contract and some minor procurement contracts Current commitment is 91% of the forecast end cost. Budget savings are confirmed. Contingency drawdown remains at all.

4.2 Actual cost to date includes payments for major equipment. No contract claims are outstanding.

4.3 Benefits capture on track.

5. **Key Risks and Issues:**

5.1 Remaining risk is now categorized as "low." Identified remaining risks are associated with site landscaping and the potential for inciement weather. This, however, will not delay the commissioning of the new site. There are no stakeholder issues.

Figure 3-5:   Program of work status report example.

The widespread adoption of project management through-out most sectors and across the world has seen the profession boom, particularly in the past couple of decades. Most, if not all, of us will have observed an abundance of new thinking, leading to new standards, tools, techniques, and processes being developed and adopted. We should also be aware that there is a huge amount of investment in training and development, with much of this leading to certifications or qualifications of some sort. However, this has come with an apparent cost; project failure rates seem to be rising. Research done by PMI and published in 2015 via the *Pulse of the Profession®: Capturing the Value of Project Management* report suggests that typical project failure rates are over 35% and have been for the past few years. This is clearly unacceptable and highlights the significant waste of money, time, and resources to the organizations directly experiencing these. This poor performance derails the organization from achieving strategic goals, business objectives, and benefits from lost opportunities.

There are many factors that contribute to projects failing, and one wonders if this is the result of a lack of forward thinking that looks beyond new tools, techniques, process, and even templates. There is a huge amount of energy being expended on promoting processes, training for certifications, and software tools. Perhaps the real clues to reducing the project failure rate are embedded in a 2005 KPMG *Global IT Project Management Survey,* which showed that organizations were conducting more projects that required more money and that were more complex. Great, one might think! Not so perhaps, as one can observe that more projects make the profession more appealing to those who are not project managers, who seek out easy-to-get project management certifications to make themselves more appealing to potential employers. Also, the "more money" mantra can seemingly offer higher income earnings to those who are involved or seek to be involved. As a consequence, the complexity and risk aspects get discounted because of lack of skill and experience, and a reliance on the processes, procedures, and templates being used. Another observation is that if one adds the three elements of project volume, money, and complexity together, there is likely to be a very significant increase in organizational risk. This is not just specific project-oriented risk embedded within scope, time, and cost, but risk associated with the organization's capability, capacity, and brand reputation. Failure at this level can lead to disgruntled stakeholders, loss of customers, decline in market share, and a negative brand image. Those using social media channels seem not to care if this brand image is real or perceived.

From this, we can begin to see that project management as a profession has itself become more complex. To be a truly great enabler of a performance lift, in terms of the overall health and well-being of your organization, there needs to be a correlation and direct linkage to program and portfolio management. Second, program of work and project practitioners need to consider professional development that is tuned to business management rather than chasing, as many seem to do, popular process-centric certifications. Finally, organizational leaders need to foster cultures that promote thinking about risk and opportunity areas within a value management framework. This would lead to more robust business case proposals, which in turn would lead to better decision making throughout the organization. All of those aspects fit well into a value-driven portfolio management organization that has a culture of nimbleness, empowerment, opportunism, and simplicity as its core values and is deployed through the 3 Ps to Success of purpose, people, and performance.

Dealing with complexity requires attention in a range of areas, not the least of which is talent management, and specifically the skill development of the resources deployed to support complex project activity. However, this is not about embarking on wholesale project management training across the organization, as this is unlikely to give a sustainable outcome. That approach is likely to cost a considerable amount of money and could well deliver a low-level result. There are two critical factors that contribute toward combatting complexity, and therefore, the downstream success of any reasonably sized project today. These, if focused on and executed well, will lay a foundation for the sustainable success of any project-based initiative. The critical factors are:

1. Organizational capability and maturity in project management, and
2. Capability and skills of project people in the organization.

The first factor requires an organization to be fully aware of its ability and capability to perform and successfully deliver any project or group of projects (program) from initiation through to completion and handover. It is vital to ensure that existing skill sets are known and mapped to project complexity level and scale. There is a number of assessment tools available today, some of which are highlighted in Section 1-6, that allow a view of capability to be determined and then mapped against the type and scale of future project work. This shows the gaps that need to be filled to reduce the risk of failure through inappropriate skill sets being deployed on projects that are highly complex or risky. Maturity assessment also requires robust and appropriate project governance to be evident and in use. Governance would include leadership and ownership, organizational structure, commercial approaches, decision making, and macro-change control. No initiative should commence without a business case that clearly demonstrates both the output (project deliverable) and the outcome (business benefit) of the proposed initiative.

In regard to the second critical factor, too often we see the development of talent being restricted to budget-controlled discretionary amounts. Mixed line management and HR views often lead to money being squandered on personalized training. Instead, training should be based on skill and knowledge development, which has specifically been assessed through a robust individual capability assessment process of reasonable (mid to high recommended) rigor, which then leads to a defined career path that contributes directly to the mission of the organization.

This attention to determining project management maturity at both the organizational and individual levels will allow those resources involved in project activity to deal with the complexity that each project or group of projects presents. Furthermore, those resources should be better able to utilize the tools and techniques within the organization at a higher level. This would include better decision making in project selection, improved project planning and delivery, as well as earlier achievement of outcomes by way of benefits realization and value enhancement. Examples include closer matching of resource capability to level of complexity and more integration of scope, time, cost, risk, and perhaps enhanced but simplified use of earned value management, a proven technique on forward-looking project performance that is underutilized because of overcomplication by some and theoretical approaches by others.

This talent management approach to dealing with complexity requires an organizational shift from the top down. A culture of support is required from project governance through to project management office units to project team members. Support and development needs to be aligned for maximum return against reducing organizational risk, reducing cost wastage, and maximizing benefits return and enhancing brand reputation—back to the four core values of nimbleness, empowerment, opportunism, and simplicity, as mentioned earlier in this section.

Program/project management offices need to advocate, and keep advocating, for competence-based learning rather than the kind of easy-to-get "memory-test" certification that, unfortunately, so many pursue.

Referring back to Section 2, leaders who adopt a portfolio management model and drive that across the whole organization to "get stuff done" could eventually drop the word *project* from the term *project management*, as a result of all work being done in an integrated and coordinated manner through matrix structures.

The classic project management elements of scope, cost, and time are still very relevant in the economic climate of today, so practitioners who have enhanced or advanced skills in those areas should be able to deal with increasing challenges and add more value to their respective organizations. However, PMI has it right in terms of its recently introduced PMI Talent Triangle®, which states that modern practitioners of the P3M profession need to have skills and experience in three areas: leadership, technical, and strategic and business management. For those involved in portfolio management, the emphasis should be on strategic and business management capability, and for those involved in program of work and project management, the focus should be on leadership. This does not mean that a person should have only just one set of skills to offer, rather, a person should have a more predominant offering that relates to the specific job he or she is performing.

The bottom line is to develop all of your talent to allow your organization to achieve a lift in performance that is sustainable and contributes directly to increased performance and organizational value.

It is not the strongest of the species that survives, nor the most intelligent, but the one that is most responsive to change.

—**Charles Darwin**

Supporting Functions: Time for Change!

4-1. Leadership in Organizations

In the post-GFC environment, leaders are being challenged to provide new and faster solutions to those market pressures referred to at the beginning of Section 1. Value-driven portfolio management needs to be better recognized as an alternative approach to traditional functional ways of conducting business. Value-driven portfolio management allows for better alignment to strategic intents as well as a nimbler organizational structure able to act on a need for change much more quickly and effectively than traditional functional practices. This requires the presence of strong portfolio management skill sets that are business focused as opposed to the predominantly delivery focus that we see in program of work and project management.

Effective and relevant leadership is critical to successful organizations, so portfolio managers, and to some degree program managers, need to acquire, develop, and utilize leadership skills to bring about change that drives increased value to the organization through their respective actions.

4-2. Leadership Role Focus

The focus, horizon, and timing can be different depending on the leadership role. Various leadership styles can be utilized during different phases of portfolio, program of work, and project management (P3M) activity, depending on the situation at any given point. It is important to accept that each of these styles has its particular place in a P3M environment. Here is a sample of principles, styles, and techniques that can be adapted to suit your focus.

The work done by author and speaker Mark Sanborn, reflected in his book *You Don't Need a Title to Be a Leader,* explains how anyone, anywhere, can make a positive difference. Sanborn offers six *principles* of leadership that, if deployed, will leave a lasting legacy. His principles are as follows:

- **Self-mastery** – You must first master yourself before you can expect to lead others.
- **Focus** – Focus and determination trump brains and brawn every time.
- **Power with people** – Managers exercise power over people, whereas leaders exercise power with people.
- **Persuasive communications** – Others tell; leaders sell.
- **Execution** – Your success depends on your implementation quotient—your ability to get things done.
- **Giving** – Leaders focus more on what they give than on what they get.

Simply put, yet powerful!

Commonly accepted *styles* from Daniel Goleman's March–April 2000 *Harvard Business Review* magazine bestseller article, "Leadership: The Power of Emotional Intelligence" are the following:

- **Pace setting** (do as I do, now)
- **Authoritative visionary** (come with me)

- **Affiliate** (people come first)
- **Coaching** (try this)
- **Democratic** (what do you think?)
- **Coercive and commanding** (do what I tell you)

A great portfolio, program of work, or project leader will utilize a blend of those styles and also change the blend recipe as the need arises.

Further success lies in the *techniques* used by portfolio, program of work, or project leaders. For example, the *HELP* approach is one I loosely adopted some years ago, and it has proved to be very useful. The *HELP* acronym stands for:

- **H** – Humor those involved;
- **E** – Excite them;
- **L** – Listen to them as appropriate; and
- **P** – Praise as often as you can and when relevant.

So, in a P3M context, portfolio managers should focus on strategic alignment and impact, investment choices, prioritization (i.e., investing in the right things), and adding value to decision making through a value management framework.

Program of work managers, however, need to focus on delivery of the outcomes and benefits, managing stakeholder relationships, conflict resolution, interdependencies, and guiding change.

At a project management level, project managers need to focus on delivery of the outputs, managing and communicating with stakeholders, and managing project team members.

All of the three leader groups must have highly developed communications and interpersonal skills as well as flexibility in their use of leadership styles, techniques, and principles.

Table 4-1 provides a leadership comparison of typical leadership traits among P3M managers.

Table 4-1:   Comparison of portfolio, program, and project managers.

Portfolio Manager	Program of Work Manager	Project Manager
Portfolio managers have high levels of business acumen, strategic insight, and value strategy synthesis.	Program managers are leaders providing vision and leadership to a defined program of work.	Project managers are team managers and players who motivate using their knowledge and skills.
Leadership style focuses on adding value to the organization via portfolio decision making and driving business results via value planning.	Leadership style focuses on managing relationships and conflict resolution to meet intended outcome via value engineering. Program managers need to facilitate and manages the political aspects of stakeholder management.	Leadership style focuses on project output delivery and activity directive in order to meet success criteria of output (i.e., value delivery).
Portfolio managers usually manage or coordinate portfolio management staff.	Program managers usually manage project managers.	Project managers usually manage technical staff, specialists, and so forth.

4-3. Influencing for Change

Change management is a term that is in constant use these days, almost to the point where it has become overused. From the original domain of HR and others, the term is now widespread across all areas of an organization, and also across a wide range of sectors. In recent years, the portfolio, program, and project management profession has also adopted the term in abundance initially to refer to activities relating to internal IT system rollout activity, but now use it when referring to activities that are far-reaching, such as organizational change on a transformational scale.

There is so much information and a fair bit of hype around change management. It seems to be akin to the buzz around benefits realization—everybody wants it, but few understand it. Indeed, with change management, it seems that everybody has a change management skill set to offer. This is probably quite true; however, it is the deep understanding of change (i.e., the need for the change, the scale of the change, and the goal of the change), that differentiates the expert from the amateur. The following pages offer a view on change that should assist leaders to guide a P3M change through their organization.

What is Change Management?

This question can be answered by sharing two quotes. First, a quote from a white paper I wrote on change titled *Change Management— Going from Good to Great*:

> Change management is a structured approach to transitioning individuals, teams, and organisations from a current state to a desired future state. (p. 2)

The second quote is from *The Change Management Pocket Guide* written by Kate Nelson and Stacy Aaron, who offer:

> Successful change management is the discipline of driving business results by changing behaviours. (p. 5)

These definitions provide clarity, as they both hint strongly at the people aspects of change and change management. We should explore that further.

Types of Change

Having an intimate understanding of the nature of the change you wish to effect and the context in which you are working is critical to determining an appropriate change strategy/plan. Embarking on a change journey without some idea of the environment puts you at an immediate disadvantage. One of the first stages in planning a change journey is to understand more about the type of change you wish to bring about, where you want to go, and how you plan to get there.

Some examples of change include organizational structure change, merger and acquisition change, IT system release, business process re-engineering change, program of work change, and project scope change. All of these present differing levels of risk and opportunity to the organization.

Not all changes will require the same level of planning or the same tools and techniques. As an example, simple change may affect many people, while complex change may only impact a small number of people. The level of change management effort, therefore, depends on two dimensions—the complexity of the change and the scale of the change. No matter what combination of these dimensions you intend to implement, there is always a degree of risk relating to the type of change.

There are three types of change that have varying levels of risk and therefore require different planning requirements:

- **Operational change** – This tends to be changes to local processes and behaviors. These tend to be departmental or localized and can be quite straightforward to implement.
- **Tactical change** – This is probably the most common type, as the business looks to continuously improve its performance and process efficiency, through organization-wide adjustments to everyday working methods.
- **Strategic change** – This kind of change is radical and usually requires the organization and its stakeholders to make a large shift from the current state. Transformation is the most extreme and far-reaching form of strategic change and can result in a future organization that differs significantly from the existing one in terms of structure, processes, culture, and sometimes product or service offerings.

It is in the larger tactical and strategic change types where leading change is most needed and could make or break the success and long-term benefits to the organization. Larger changes can be either proactive (let's improve) or reactive (let's fight back). Sometimes, it can be a combination of both. However, today it needs to be predominantly proactive in order to stay ahead.

Four Conditions for Change

Successful organizational change occurs when the senior executives convince employees not only to absorb change, but to commit to it. This should be done via a change sponsor and a change leader.

To gain this commitment, change leaders must strive to achieve the following:

- Staff see their leadership actively modeling and advocating for the change.
- Staff have the skills to do what is required of them in the future.
- Staff alter their mind-set because they see the point of the change, can see what it means for them, and agree with it.
- The surrounding structures, processes, and reward systems are in place to support the change objective.

People and Change

Organizational change is often difficult for staff and other stakeholders to accept. However, understanding why the change is happening, and what it means for them personally, can dramatically increase their receptiveness to the change. In addition, the confusion and fear experienced by staff during and after a major change event can be significantly reduced if the change is well planned and well managed.

Successful organizational change occurs when the change leader has convinced staff and others not only to absorb the change but to commit to it.

Approaches to Change

Change management has evolved from the domain of psychologists, HR people, and "touchy-feely" types who seemed to talk about intangibles and at the same time lacked accountability, thereby hampering change management from becoming a recognized business discipline.

Recently, change management has experienced a paradigm shift away from the bolted-on "change consultant" model toward the creation of an integrated, structured approach that delivers tangible and measurable value to strategic as well as tactical business activity. Change management is seen by some as the application of two converging and predominant fields of thought: a hard-wired engineering approach to improving business performance and the soft-skill psychological approach to managing the human side of change. Understanding and managing this convergence of thought is seen as essential for successful business change in today's environment.

Forming an intimate understanding of the scope and scale of your planned change will guide you toward the most suitable approach or combination of approaches. The following approaches to change are common:

- **Engineering approach** – This approach looks at how to make changes to the operations of a business as a mechanical system. It focuses on observable, measurable business elements that can be changed or improved. Historically, companies with a mechanical view do not value change management concepts. They do, however, value the result and the ongoing continuous improvement effort that is required.
- **Psychological approach** – Here, the emphasis is on how humans react to their environment and to change. Change management is concerned with helping individuals "make sense" of what the change means to them personally.
- **Process approach** – Harvard Professor John Kotter has written widely on change. His book *Leading Change* (1996) outlines an actionable eight-step process for implementing successful transformations.
- **Being-versus-doing approach** – In his book *Powerful Conversations: How High Impact Leaders Communicate* (1999), author Phil Harkins says that leaders influence cultural change not only through memos and meetings, but also through the many one-to-one conversations they hold throughout a day. What makes a conversation powerful is that all those involved share important feelings, ideas, and beliefs. Conversations

must be planned and managed with the focus on "being the change," and the doing of the change will happen as a result.

- **Skills-based approach** – Rosabeth Moss Kanter, in her book *The Enduring Skills of Change Leaders* (1999), states that change-adept organizations share three attributes: the imagination to innovate, the professionalism to perform, and the openness to collaborate. The most important things a leader can bring to a changing organization are passion, conviction, and instilling confidence in others. Too often, executives announce a change initiative, launch a task force, and then simply hope that people find the answers. Instead, they should be offering a dream, stretching their horizons, and encouraging people to do the same.

- **Storytelling approach** – In her book *The Story Factor* (2006), Annette Simmons notes that stories make points in less confrontational ways than arguments. The message can be put out and left for the individual to ponder. Stories are powerful because they touch the emotions as well as the mind in a memorable way. Changing a diametrically opposed opinion would require you to move in a "baby-step" manner. A story gives you the perfect format to gradually and indirectly move someone from one end of a continuum to the other.

The above is not intended to be a list from which you would select a single approach. In reality, a combination of these approaches is likely. This combination will fluctuate as the phases of the change initiative are implemented and as staff commit to the change.

Change management is not a forgiving process. It must have a well-thought-out and clear objective and implementation plan. However, as you uncover more information and as assumptions and issues are challenged and resolved, you will need to revalidate ambiguities and demonstrate degrees of leadership courage in guiding and managing stakeholders to move forward. The most successful change initiatives are those that have a plan that goes beyond the implementation mechanics of the change, and a comprehensive view on how to sustain the change via people.

Change in a Merger and Acquisition Environment

Mergers, post-acquisition or otherwise, are often done to reduce costs, rationalize or increase numbers, and so on, to achieve economies of scale and growth. It is vital, therefore, that leaders articulate the vision for the new organization and how it is to proceed, rather than just its business outputs.

A successful merger should not be a marriage of existing organizations, but a new birth from separate cultures—a different and single culture is the goal. It may be a mistake to take the best from both cultures and attempt to bolt them together to create something new, as this is likely to fail because of conflicting legacy values. Change managers should recognize that a merger is not simply the joining of separate organizations, but actually the creation of a brand-new one. This presents opportunities that should be exploited and not overlooked. Start by exploring or creating the core values of the new organization. By doing this, the staff of the respective merged organizations will likely identify with the values of their existing entities anyway, but with a view to what they share rather than what is different across the new organization. Subsequent change planning and its implementation should be easier with this shared new set of values.

A couple of points to remember and integrate into any merger change plan are:

- Organizations of professionals (e.g., health, education, engineers, lawyers, etc.) are more likely to resist a merger, as they may see it as a criticism of their learning, practices, and outputs, and therefore, their profession as a whole; and
- Organizations are generally communities of people, not products, systems, or processes. The stronger the

association with the views of the community and its direction and values, the more resistance the community will be to change, and to a merger, in particular. People view change in terms of what will happen to them first and then to their community.

The Magic Ingredient?

It was tempting to create a list of magic ingredients, but I have decided to offer just one. It's the trait of *leadership courage*, sometimes referred to as managerial courage. To me, having this trait combats the notion of change leaders being too soft to succeed by not making decisions, or taking too long to make decisions, for fear of upsetting people.

A number of factors differentiate the consistently successful change leader, and these revolve around the cultural and physiological makeup of the change leader. The ability to influence others is inherent within them.

Here are six questions to test leadership courage traits:

- Do you avoid making strong decisions because they may upset some people?
- Do you hold back from providing constructive criticism?
- Do you avoid escalating to change sponsor or higher level?
- Are you demanding excellence in the execution of the change program?
- Are you holding staff accountable?
- Are you doing too much work yourself?

If you have answered the above with more "yeses" than "nos," then you may already have good levels of leadership courage. Though not scientific, your answers will provide a guide as to where you may wish to invest in some skill development. Change management is not for the faint of heart—it requires the head, heart, and gut (or judgment) all to be present and aligned.

Footnote on Change

In summary, then, there are three absolute focus areas that sponsors and leaders of change should prioritize: the change leader's capability, the state of mind within the organization, and the process utilized to enact the change. Many organizations put the change management process as the priority. No wonder there are failures!

Stakeholder management is also key to successful organizational change—program of work plans developed for the implementation of the change need to demonstrate an understanding of, and integration with, generally accepted methods of organizational change management.

Consider the words and message of 20th-century American author Kurt Vonnegut:

> *Of all the words of mice and men, the saddest are, it might have been.*

Perhaps he was influenced by the great 18th-century Scottish bard and poet Robert Burns, who when toiling in a field, wrote:

> *The best laid plans of mice and men go aft agley.* (The best laid plans of mice and men go often wrong.)

Today's risk-averse cultures are perhaps stagnating, or at least slowing, decisions surrounding change at the tactical and strategic levels. Too often, there is much negativity surrounding risk, which results in the flip side of risk—that is, opportunity being underanalyzed or even overlooked.

Referring back to the great words from Vonnegut and Burns, we need to be more receptive and welcoming of change and of the opportunities associated with risk as we strive to make our organizations future ready.

The Art of Influencing

This is where the storytelling ability and skill of a change leader become really obvious. A critical skill is a leader's ability to articulate his or her vision as well as the organization's vision, and to clearly communicate plans to others. Going back to Mark Sanborn's list of leadership principles, it is the ability to utilize the "persuasive communications" skill to effectively rally the organization and thereby set the combined direction.

I had an interesting discussion recently where I was asked by a well-respected professional colleague about the differences between influence and "office politics." This got me thinking and I responded by stating that influence is measured, sincere, and compassionate, whereas office politics may be measured, but lacks the other two traits. I still hold this view.

So, what is influence? In his book *The 21 Irrefutable Laws of Leadership* (1998), author John Maxwell nailed it in Law #2, by stating:

> The true measure of leadership is influence—nothing more, nothing less. (p. 11)

This quote captures and provides clarity on the importance of influence. In Section 3, we also discussed that influence is the degree of power a person has to exert on a program of work. This can be positive or negative. It also applies to portfolio and project management.

Steps in Influencing

Influence is not something that just happens by accident, and it is more than just communication. To be successful in your ability to influence, there are four key steps that can assist in most situations:

Step 1 – Prepare

- Identify the desired outcomes.
- Identify the key stakeholders.
- Develop the key messages.
- Plan carefully—time, place, people, risks, and so on.

Step 2 – Create a Connection (Develop Rapport)

- Highlight factors you have in common.
- Display empathy.
- Develop trust.
- Acknowledge mutual credibility.

Step 3 – Assess Other People's Needs and Values

- Demonstrate genuine concern for other people's viewpoints.
- Listen and note.
- Incorporate as appropriate.

Step 4 – Be Persuasive

- Don't stop, don't give up, and be assertive.
- Communicate often.
- Reinforce messages constantly.

These steps, executed in a genuine manner using a combination of head, heart, and gut, will greatly assist you in being seen and considered a person with influence.

4-4. Portfolio Management Office

It is important to note that portfolio management offices can have different purposes, and the drivers behind the need for one will dictate what functions it should perform. The level of P3M maturity of your organization will influence the portfolio management office's ability to function consistently, add real value, and operate at a high-performance level.

The purpose and scope of a portfolio management office may vary considerably, as well as its degree of influence. For example, it can be a repository of information or a support function to portfolio, program of work, and project managers by providing assistance to their roles. For a portfolio management office that focuses on the portfolio level, the purpose should be to assist in developing and supporting the implementation of business strategies throughout the organization. When doing this, aspects to consider should include:

- The portfolio management office is actively engaged in value planning associated with the crafting and definition of strategy and related portfolios;
- The portfolio management office should support other teams by handling some administrative and other functions centrally and at an organizational level;
- The portfolio management office is responsible for tracking and confirming benefits from program of work and project activity. This responsibility would be on the executive sponsor in the extended role of benefits owner;
- The portfolio management office would provide support to *all* programs of work. This portfolio management office would essentially be an enterprise model (i.e., an EPMO); and
- The portfolio management office may be established to define and manage specific related governance processes, procedures, templates, and so forth, with which all programs of work must comply.

If your organization currently has a low level of P3M maturity, then a portfolio management office should focus on setting and ensuring that work methods/frameworks for program of work and project execution are available and being consistently used. It will also provide process support to the various people involved in program of work and project activity. Professional development, resource management, and other function areas can be added once higher levels of maturity are achieved.

Figure 4-1 shows a number of general functions for which a portfolio management office can be responsible. This is not intended to be a definitive list, nor is it mandatory for all portfolio management offices to achieve or undertake them.

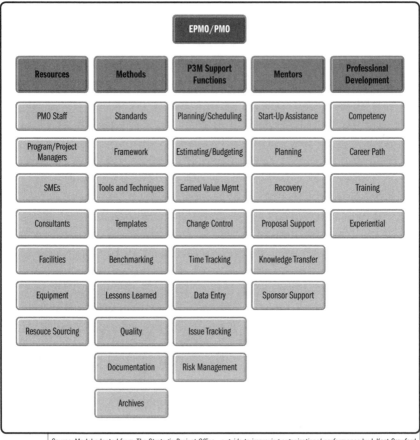

Source: Model adapted from *The Strategic Project Office - a guide to improving organizational performance* by J. Kent Crawford

Figure 4-1: EPMO/portfolio management office function options.

An important point to consider here is that different models of portfolio management offices will have different focuses and functions. For example, a portfolio focus is more strategic (i.e., around the achievement of goals and objectives), whereas a project focus is more tactical, and therefore, focused on delivery of outputs.

Each organization must look at its own needs in the context of P3M maturity and whether or not portfolio management is being utilized in its true sense, and then design and implement the supporting office functions as necessary.

4-5. Portfolio Manager's Responsibility and Expertise

Portfolio Manager's Responsibility

A good portfolio manager will typically be, or have been, a senior manager with a demonstrated understanding of execution against goals and objectives. The portfolio manager manages assigned portfolios in the following ways:

- Plays a key role in prioritization, ensuring balance of components and alignment with strategic objectives;
- Provides key stakeholders with periodic assessment of the portfolio and its performance, plus early identification of issues and risks impacting performance and achievability;
- Measures the value to the organization through investment value management, use of balanced scorecard, and other financial-oriented measurements, such as return on investment (ROI), net present value (NPV), and so on; also meets legislative mandates, implementing policy, and so on;
- Ensures timely and consistent communication to stakeholders on progress, impacts, and changes associated with the management of each portfolio to maintain stakeholder understanding and support of the objectives and approach desired; and
- Participates in program and, if necessary, project reviews to reflect senior-level support, leadership, and involvement in important matters.

Portfolio Manager's Expertise

To succeed in their responsibility, portfolio managers should have adequate experience and expertise in:

- Developing a deep understanding of the organization's vision, mission, and strategy to aid in optimizing each portfolio;

- Understanding how to relate strategic goals, objectives, and priorities within each portfolio to contribute toward the organization's goals and objectives;
- Strong leadership traits that display a mix of style, technique, and principles;
- General management acumen (i.e., experience and knowledge) of:
  - Interpersonal and communication skills to interact with senior management;
  - Relevant markets, customer base, other stakeholders, standards, and the regulatory environment;
  - Business unit management; and
  - Leadership courage.
- Business process development and continuous improvement theories;
- Benefits realization management, both fiscal and nonfiscal;
- Development of appropriate portfolio management processes;
- High-level and, if required, detailed reporting to determine the health of each portfolio and respective components; and
- Program of work and project management methods and techniques.

The key point to consider here is that, contrary to the belief by some, neither the role of a portfolio manager nor the function of portfolio management is a "rite of passage" career path step for program of work and project leaders and practitioners.

4-6. Program Manager's Responsibility and Expertise

Program Manager's Responsibility

Typically, a program of work manager is responsible for:

- Managing programs of work with activities that may span functions, organizations, geographic regions, and cultures;

- Continually checking alignment of program scope with strategic business objectives and recommending changes to enhance business results;
- Stakeholder engagement at multiple levels, internal and external to the organization;
- Determining and coordination of resources among component projects;
- Monitoring projects and ongoing work and reporting through governance structures; and
- Ensuring the ultimate success and acceptance of the program of work.

Program Manager's Expertise

Typically, a program of work manager will have many years of experience in managing large projects or multiprojects with varying levels of complexity. To succeed in their responsibility, program managers need expertise and experience in:

- Program management;
- Benefits realization management, both fiscal and nonfiscal;
- Finance and cost management principles;
- Cross-cultural awareness, both internal and external to the organization;
- Leadership and managerial courage;
- Strong communication skills;
- Ability to influence others;
- Negotiation and decision making;
- Conflict resolution; and
- Project management in business or government environments.

Program of work managers can aspire toward a portfolio role as they develop their leadership and business acumen skills. Naturally, program of work managers usually make good managers of large and complex projects.

4-7. Qualifications and Credentials Options

Professional qualifications and credentials can support the human talent growth and maturity of any organization. They serve to provide knowledge of common standards, procedures, lexicon, and best practices.

Educational qualifications are a separate form of recognition of ability. However, it should always be remembered that a qualification does not guarantee a certification. *Certification* is the term used by many professional institutes to recognize individuals who have attained a certain professional standard. Those who have achieved the required standard, in accordance with established criteria, are eligible to receive a "certificate," hence, the term.

Certification designations assist in career advancement by providing an opportunity to pursue continuing education, increase involvement in the profession, and receive industry-wide recognition. However, a certificate alone may not necessarily equip people with the necessary skills to manage complex portfolios or programs of work. The same can apply to projects that are highly complex and have other challenging attributes. Conducting individual capability assessments will allow for accurate benchmarking of each person's capability level and also identify what skill and knowledge training he or she might need.

Below is a selection of organizations that offer portfolio and program management certifications.

Australian Institute of Project Management (AIPM) offers national, international, and organizational credentials. These are offered through the institute's Registered Project Manager (RegPM) national certificate program. It involves an individually designed competency-based workplace assessment program. Candidates are required to compile evidence that displays their competence in project management. The RegPM certificate is awarded at one of five levels, as shown below:

> **Certified Practising Portfolio Executive (CPPE):** The portfolio executive monitors a series of projects and

evaluates which ones are most beneficial in light of the whole organization's strategy.

Certified Practising Project Director (CPPD): This level suits those who regularly direct projects, assess whether progress is in line with organizational goals, and analyze effectiveness.

Certified Practising Senior Project Manager (CPSPM): The senior project manager is the go-to person who manages difficult and high-risk projects that have the potential to impact the organization and key stakeholders.

There are two other certificates that have been omitted from this text, as they are project management practitioner oriented.

For details of the full range of AIPM offerings, visit its website at www.aipm.com.au/certification.

AXELOS: AXELOS specializes in the accreditation and certification of organizations, processes, and people within a range of industries and management disciplines. They offer the MoP, MSP, PRINCE2, and other process certification schemes, via approved agents. Previously, this was done via the Office of Government Commerce (OGC) in the United Kingdom:

Management of Portfolios (MoP®): This provides universally applicable principles and practices that will enable individuals and organizations to successfully introduce or re-energize portfolio management approaches. There are currently two qualification levels available—MoP Foundation and MoP Practitioner.

Managing Successful Programs (MSP®): This comprises a set of principles and processes for use when managing a program. It is founded on best practice, although it is not prescriptive. There are currently two qualification levels available—MSP Foundation and MSP Practitioner.

AXELOS also has PRINCE2® and other offerings. Although they are good credentials, they are not included here, as their focus is primarily on project managers and project team members.

For details of the full range of AXELOS offerings, visit its website at www.axelos.com/certifications.

International Project Management Association (IPMA) is an international network of national project management societies. IPMA owns and maintains its universal system for validating project management qualification and competence programs on a global basis. Each member association is responsible for developing and managing its own project management qualification and competence products and for establishing its bodies for certification. Each membership association agrees to participate in IPMA's validation procedure.

IPMA coordinates and harmonizes the various qualification and competence programs of the member associations through four levels:

Level A: Certified Projects Director: Has at least five years of experience in project portfolio management, program management, or multiproject management, of which three years is in responsible leadership functions in the portfolio management of a company/organization (or a branch), or in the management of important programs.

Level B: Certified Senior Project Manager: Has at least five years of project management experience, of which three years are in responsible leadership functions of complex projects.

Level C: Certified Project Manager: Has at least three years of project management experience in responsible leadership functions of projects with limited complexity.

Level D: Certified Project Management Associate: Experience in the project management competence elements is not compulsory, but it is an advantage if the candidate has applied his or her project management knowledge to some extent already.

For details on the full range of IPMA offerings, visit its website at www.ipma.world/certification.

Project Management Institute (PMI): The preparation process for each of PMI's certifications differs, but always requires some practical experience and includes intensive study and an examination. Each certification also requires adherence to a defined Code of Ethics and Professional Conduct.

Portfolio Management Professional (PfMP)®: This is PMI's certification designed to demonstrate portfolio management skills and experience. To be eligible for the PfMP® certification, the candidate must meet specific guidelines that objectively measure experience, education, and professional knowledge, and undergo a rigorous application process as well an assessment phase. Other PMI certifications are not prerequisites for the PfMP certification.

Program Management Professional (PgMP)®: This is PMI's certification designed to demonstrate program management skills and experience. To be eligible for the PgMP® certification, a candidate must meet specific guidelines that objectively measure experience, education, and professional knowledge, and undergo a rigorous application process as well as three assessments. Other PMI certifications are not prerequisites for the PgMP certification.

PMI also has its Project Management Professional (PMP)® and Certified Associate in Project Management (CAPM)® and other offerings. Though they are very good certifications, they are not included here, because their focus is primarily on project managers and project team members.

For details on the full range of PMI offerings, visit its website at www.pmi.org/certification.

4-8. Ongoing Improvement

The successful and sustainable use of value management and portfolio management needs to evolve with the organization's leadership, P3M maturity, capability, and changes to its culture and environment. With most new approaches adopted within an organization, ongoing reviews of performance are a key factor to improvement. Once value management and portfolio management structures are in place and operating, regular reviews should be conducted to ensure that they meet the needs for which they were established, and new needs if further change has been instigated.

These reviews should include a cross-section selection of stakeholders who are/will be affected by the change. This might include senior management, portfolio and program of work managers, team members, stakeholders, and so on. Feedback survey instruments are useful tools, as are review meetings. Whatever approach or approaches are used, the key to success is clearly stating the objectives and considering the feedback received as constructive to ongoing improvement.

It is important to note, as per a long-standing adage, that *you can please some of the people some of the time, but not all of the people all of the time*, so it's likely that you will never meet all stakeholder expectations. The establishment of sensible metrics at the beginning will greatly assist in managing expectations, as well as maintaining a portfolio management system that is appropriate to the needs of the organization. An integrated and connected organization will allow for change drivers to be identified early, thus allowing the organization to respond early and thereby capitalize early as a result.

EPMO/PMO Performance Monitoring

When you began the process of implementing a portfolio management approach and structure, you will have created a Terms of Reference, Charter, or something similar. Refer back to this document to ensure that you are still on track with what was originally envisioned. Changes to original objectives should be discussed, noted, and authorized by the sponsor of the initiative where appropriate.

Here is a sample of questions that can be adapted to assist in the review analysis of data and other feedback collected:

- Has overall organizational performance improved?
- Have sponsors maintained or increased their commitment?
- Are executives satisfied with the information they are receiving in order to make better business decisions?
- Is there evidence of a cultural change toward the support of a value-driven portfolio management approach to business?
- Are programs of work and projects aligned with business objectives and prioritized by value contribution?
- How well is value management being used?
- How well is portfolio management being supported by an EPMO or something similar?
- Is periodic surveying of key stakeholders (e.g., satisfaction with process, performance perceptions, and performance improvements)?
- Is the EPMO/PMO regularly collecting and analyzing key performance metrics, such as return on investment, key performance indicators, failure rates, overruns, overspends, and so forth?
- Does the organization consistently use the existing framework and associated templates, standards, and processes to assist program of work and project managers in their day-to-day activities?

EPMO/PMO Scalability

Enterprise portfolio management offices (EPMOs), portfolio management offices, and program management offices need to be scalable to suit changing business needs. For example:

- A portfolio's content can be changed to accommodate changing strategy or changes to related strategic goals and business objectives;

- A collective of programs of work can become a new portfolio;
- A small program of work or individual project management office can be scaled up to become a larger and more comprehensive program management office; and
- A large program of work can be reduced in size to accommodate a decrease in scope, priority, or value.

It is important to be able to recognize when this scaling should take place. Clear indications that could assist in recognizing the need for scaling might include:

- Changes in the economic environment requiring the organization to reprioritize capital and operational expenditure. Remember the continuum of investment model shown in Section 1-2 (Figure 1-1). The EPMO/PMO would scale up or down depending on any rebalancing of funds when compared to the value contributed or change demand;
- When a portfolio or program of work manager is looking for ways to improve work flow by delivering more outputs and outcomes faster and for less cost using the same resources;
- Existence of a project overload situation that increases resource demand beyond current capacity; and
- Rebalancing and reprioritizing portfolio content to achieve better program of work/project mix. This could include deleting some work so that a lesser number of projects contributes a larger portion toward business objectives.

Once you have recognized that you need to change the scale of your EPMO/PMO, you should begin to plan for the scaling by:

- Revisiting the Terms of Reference, Charter, and so on to assess whether it is still appropriate;

- Considering where in the organizational structure the EPMO/PMO should sit and what modified governance, resourcing, and reporting are required; and
- Planning and communicating the scaling, which, in essence, is a change initiative to those key stakeholder groups identified previously and any new ones.

A tool that I found useful when assessing client needs is what I call a key function/services library. This is based on value management thinking, where EPMO or PMO key functions and corresponding services are listed. It is useful in avoiding duplication, providing clarity, and for allocating responsibility and urgency.

Skill Development

It is vital to encourage ongoing professional development of those involved in value, portfolio, program of work, or project management. It is also vital to encourage a culture of talent management and development within the organization that seeks to grow, attract, retain, and connect talent at all levels of the organizational structure. This includes those new to the organization via recent recruitment as well as selected contractors who have been engaged.

There are two critical factors that contribute to the success of any value-driven portfolio management implementation initiative, and, if focused on and executed well, will lay a foundation for sustainable success:

1. Organizational capability and maturity in portfolio and program of work and project management, and
2. Capability and skills of the people in P3M roles in organization.

The organizational capability and maturity factor requires an organization to be fully aware of its ability and capability to perform and deliver any portfolio management approach successfully. Making sure that existing skill sets are known and mapped to portfolio type and scale is vital, as are the frameworks and methods used to deliver each portfolio. Maturity also requires robust and appropriate P3M governance to be evident and in use. This includes leadership and ownership, organizational structure, steering groups, commercial approaches, decision making, and macro-change control. No program of work initiative should commence without a form of business case that clearly demonstrates both the output (project deliverables) and the outcomes (business benefits) of the proposed program of work. Projects that are to be completed without being part of a program of work must have both output and outcome clearly stated in the business case(s).

In regard to the second critical factor, too often we see the development of talent management restricted to budget-controlled discretionary amounts. Mixed line management and HR views often lead to money being squandered on personalized training. Rather, it should be skill and knowledge development that is part of a defined career path and that contributes directly to the mission of the organization.

This ongoing professional development and learning could be achieved in many ways, such as:

- Attendance and/or participation in seminars;
- Assignment of management roles to broaden experience;
- One-on-one or group coaching and/or mentoring;
- Formal training in diploma, degree, or certifications; and
- Immersing and involvement in an actual program of work or project work experience.

The bottom line is to develop your talent to allow your organization to achieve a lift in performance that is sustainable and contributes directly to sustained higher levels of performance.

Issues and Constraints

This section offers some thoughts and views on the potential issues and constraints in adopting a value-driven portfolio management business model and changing the culture across your organization.

As discussed earlier in Section 4-3, the introduction and acceptance of change, especially associated with new structures and ways of working, can be a difficult process for individuals, groups, and leaders alike. Several issues and constraints are likely to arise when introducing value and portfolio management to your organization. Based on my own experiences, Table 4-2 outlines some common issues that may arise in your situation. Hopefully, these will allow you to consider, analyze, and develop countermeasures against each, so that your change management plan is adaptive, sustainable, and of value to your organization—both in the near term and in the medium to longer terms.

Table 4-2: Issues and constraints table.

Category	Shared Issue/Constraint	Specific to Portfolio Management	Specific to Program Management
Political	Organization politics prevent full implementation.	Inclusion of "pet" projects, which fall outside the value planning criteria.	Perceived ownership of a resource(s).
Economic	Costly to put the necessary infrastructure in place.	Unclear prioritization criteria.	Takes time to realize the monetary benefits (e.g., ROI).
Social/Cultural	The P3M framework/methodology is not widely used.	Portfolio managers are not accustomed to working cross-functionally.	Teams are unaccustomed to sharing knowledge about their program of work content.
Technological	Current software systems will not support a portfolio management change.	There is a variety of software packages used throughout the organization.	One big schedule is unmanageable using existing tools.
Legal	Corporate governance fails to see the value.	P3M governance has no provision for this.	Confusion via contract-driven (outsourced) programs of work.
Environmental	Model is not adapted to the suit the organization or sector environment.	Change in strategic direction requires a review of portfolio structure.	There is no consistent reporting.
Learning	Lack of advanced P3M tertiary teaching at the university level.	Staff are generally not taught portfolio management; confusion exists.	Confusion between program of work and project management remains.

4-9. On Finance, Information Technology, Human Resources, and Legal

Finance

In today's ever-changing business environment, it is critical that finance leaders and their staff accept that value can be created, enhanced, and protected by means other than money. To this end, finance needs to be strongly integrated into other areas of the business structure. This is critical in a matrix structure.

Where an organization is considering some form of transformational activity, the opportunity for finance to add more value to the organization by being the custodians of the value management framework that is being used and by using it in conjunction with the EPMO unit, who may well be the custodians of the portfolio management framework, is large indeed. This requires a simplification of the traditional, often software-driven, chart of accounts structure, and then blending that with P3M-oriented control/cost account coding structures.

An organization that can blend finance with the EPMO and those involved with strategic planning (sometimes referred to as policy and planning) will be an organization that can reduce waste and duplication, optimize investments (both opex and capex), and set up the organization to deliver maximum value capture. Critical to making this happen is finance having an understanding of what portfolio management can be and how it uses program of work and project management.

Greater use of balanced scorecards, trending information, and integrated systems, together with simplified finance coding structures, will greatly assist in an easier transformation and streamlined understanding throughout the whole organization. However, getting finance to see the need for the change could be tough, as cautioned, somewhat tongue in cheek, by Tom Peters as the "tyranny of the bean counters."

Information Technology (IT)

Within many IT business units around the world, great debates take place over which approach to project management should be taken. Agile versus waterfall is one of the more common dialogues to be heard. Of course, IT has many interpretations, but they usually revolve around software development, system support, or a combination of those. Matching this activity to a project management approach is a well-talked-about decision that often seems to be made without great evidence to support it. Nevertheless, IT project professionals need to remind themselves that they are probably not the only business group within the organization that uses P3M techniques. It is best that the organization focus on a single chosen P3M approach and its supporting framework/tools/systems. This allows the organization to adopt a "one-voice" mantra in terms of portfolio, program of work, and project management, so that consistency of approach is maintained across the organization.

When advising the organization on which P3M systems might be suitable, it is critical to think about the level of P3M maturity that exists today and where the organization wishes to be in the near term. The volume of portfolios, programs of work, and projects undertaken; the degree of complexity associated with those; and the level of P3M capability should all be factors that guide the organization to make the right decision. A general rule of thumb is that the closer to true portfolio management adoption the organization is, the more integrated a system it will need.

It is critical to provide business systems that really suit the level of maturity and changing needs of the organization as well as to advise on and provide systems and tools that suit the desired future state of the organization. This is vital if value-driven portfolio management is to be successful in terms of facilitating and planning for the maximum value to be delivered.

Human Resources (HR)

HR professionals and their leaders have a fantastic opportunity to add considerable value to their respective organizations if they change some of the areas that seem to permeate today's focus on annual performance reviews, low-cost recruitment, and budget-controlled learning. The answer lies in HR being the custodians of the organization's culture, even if the culture is being set or driven by the executive leaders.

Referring back to the 3 Ps to Success that were discussed in Section 1-7, HR should assist the organization to formulate its purpose on talent management. HR should also advance their thinking and practice of attracting, developing, and retaining talent that is matched and suitable to the P3M capability levels evident today, and critically, to those required for the near-term future. Supporting policy needs to have clear and strong guidance on resource accountabilities and responsibilities, especially if a form of matrix structure is being adopted. Furthermore, the seeming emphasis on annual performance reviews in order to meet compliance needs that is so prevalent today needs to be rethought, scrapped, or possibly replaced with a more integrated system that blends into the adoption of P3M practices.

A relatively straightforward potential gain is that of talent retention. The answer lies in organizations making themselves as attractive as they can be to the talent that exists today. This is more than branding or marketing. The attraction aspects need to be multifaceted and clearly demonstrate to the potential resource the elements of excitement and empowerment, developmental opportunities, career path options, and entrepreneurial extras. All this needs to be conveyed through different technologies that reach and resonate with today's highly mobile and tech-savvy global gypsies. This will also require those organizations seeking resources to make additional provisions in budgets for more elaborate reward and retention programs that go beyond traditional bonus-type systems.

HR needs to be at the top leadership table of the organization, to assist other leaders in making the right decisions in regard to the adoption of value-driven portfolio management as a method to implement of their strategy. The use of capability assessments on individuals that gauge their suitability to manage complex work activity relating to value management, portfolio management, program of work, and project management is a surefire method of truly assessing what you have versus what you need.

So, in summary, ongoing improvement in the context of this section is not just about incremental change here and there. It's more toward a transformational direction, where the organization's most senior leaders show the way by creating the new structure, embracing value and portfolio management as the key mechanisms to get the "right stuff done," raising capability and empowering people, and aligning the supporting business units so that the whole organization, not just IT or operations, becomes a lot more successful at what could be called strategic implementation management.

Legal

In-house legal professionals also have an opportunity to embrace and facilitate the organization to change from its current structure, style, and culture to a desired future model. Implementing a value-driven portfolio management framework with perhaps a matrix structure is not easy and much harder if the folks in legal do not embrace and assist the advancement of the organization. An example is in corporate risk, where new approaches that embrace and encourage quick, informed opportunism are sought. Another example is the use of incentive-based contract methods, rather than the so-often-seen penalty-based contracts throughout the organization's supply chain, particularly where preferred suppliers are used. The legal minds must work hard to create new ways of conducting business that are in line with the organization's desire to change, to speed up, to react quicker, while at the same time reducing waste and risk—not easy perhaps, but certainly not impossible. CEOs need to demonstrate leadership courage and insist that the legal staff contribute positively toward the new vision of the organization.

Epilogue

Meeting the market mantras of "better, faster, cheaper" and "doing more for less" is not a one-off exercise. Organizations will need to adapt and change faster and more often than in the past, as the global economy builds and the markets expand. Further free trade agreements among various countries are examples of trade barriers being dismantled to allow more open and freer trade among nations. Global markets and new opportunities— you bet!

Becoming a high-performing organization and sustaining that requires a change in vision, in culture, in talent, and in approaches to executing business strategy. Portfolio management that is effective and well led can, together with its siblings of program and project management, provide real benefits in a number of ways, such as:

- Greater return on money spent (both capital and operational);
- Increased competiveness as a result of nimbleness;
- Increased profitability and/or productivity;
- Increased brand awareness and reputation;
- More satisfied, and therefore retained, talent;
- Healthy culture throughout the organization; and
- Engaged and informed governance levels.

One word could summarize all of the above—*value.*

The desire to change and the elements of change are possibly the most difficult to implement. Thus, keeping the overall approach as simple as possible is the key to success.

Case Study

For inspiration, here is an example of what the Government of Samoa in the South Pacific did on 8 September 2009, to change driving from the right to the left side of the road.

Here is the official summary of what happened:

At 04:00, all radio and TV channels began broadcasting reminders.

At 05:30, the Reverend Oka Fauolo, chair of the National Council of Churches, offered a prayer.

At 05:50, all vehicles had to stop and remain idle for 10 minutes.

At 06:00, everyone was to drive to the other side of the road and wait another 10 minutes.

At 06:10, everyone was to drive on.

Wonderfully simple, yet hugely effective and successful, despite many citizens expressing a fear of change.

I wrote this book for a range of reasons centered on a dream, personal reflections, and the desire to share. The approaches described in this book will offer benefits to all organizations—profit and nonprofit alike.

Focus on the 3 Ps to Success: purpose, people, and performance, along with a value-driven portfolio management framework. Leaders who can embrace the notion of simplicity within those core themes and drive strategic alignment, which is central to portfolio management, will reap the greatest benefits—both monetary and nonmonetary.

Those benefits will most likely include some or perhaps all of the following:

- Faster implementation of strategy via improved prioritization and coordination of business activity;

- Financial gain via reduced internal cost, improved efficiency, and greater return on investment (ROI);
- Improved and more effective change management;
- Earlier capture of the value that is delivered from higher performance;
- Increased understanding by all of organizational purpose via strategic goals and business objectives;
- Increased accountability, plus monitoring of all initiatives;
- Opportunity to balance short-term and longer-term investments with ongoing cost;
- Reduced risk, as interdependencies among business plan investments are more visible and better managed; and
- Competitive advantage via earlier and more informed opportunity leveraging.

However, to get these benefits requires a change from what is being done today. Do not be afraid of this, but embrace it as the new normal. Many years ago, Mahatma Gandhi shared a vision of the future: "Be the change that you wish to see in the world." You could substitute the last word for "organization," or better still, your own brand name.

Your organization's future success will not be achieved from luck, current market position, or technology. Your future success will come via leadership courage that drives change toward a value-driven portfolio management success story. You will become one of the small number of organizations that can demonstrate high levels of success in devising and implementing your strategy.

Never stop, good fortune, and I wish you every success!

Glossary

Accountable: personally responsible for an activity. Accountability cannot be delegated, unlike responsibility.

Benefits management plan: a document that reflects the planning on what benefits are expected from an initiative, when they are expected, how they are measured, who measures them, and over what period they are captured.

Benefits realization: also referred to as benefits management. The process of identifying, defining, tracking, and realizing benefits from investments made in a sustainable manner that contribute to business objectives.

Business as usual (BAU): a term applied to describe operational work conducted that is not part of a portfolio. An example is payroll.

Business case: a business document outlining the approval justification for an investment as well as its intended return or benefit.

Business objectives: specific and relatively short-term business targets. Usually derived from strategic objectives or goals.

Business value: a term used to express the entire value of an organization's business activity.

Capability: the result expected or confirmed from a measure or an assessment that is benchmarked.

Capex: capital expenditure. Provisions for creating new value or enhancing existing value.

Change management: the process of managing change from a current state toward a desired future state.

Contingency: see Reserve.

Corporate governance: the ongoing activity of setting and maintaining a sound system of direction and control by the directors and officers of an organization to ensure that effective management systems have been put in place to protect assets, earning capacity, related value, and the reputation of the organization.

Culture: a shared view on organizational well-being that revolves around policy, people, and performance.

Current state: used in capability assessments or change initiatives. Describes the "as of now" status of the organization or group of people.

Enterprise portfolio management office (EPMO): a group that provides a high-level business supporting function to the organization as a whole. Could support value management and portfolio management.

Future state: a forward-planned state of an organization, as planned by a change strategy.

Integrated reporting: business reporting that presents performance updates on P3M activity and that uses the same data source.

Key performance indicator (KPI): A metric, either financial or nonfinancial, that is used to set and measure progress toward an organizational objective.

Leadership courage: a set of attributes that a good leader displays and uses in various combinations to drive decision making, problem solving, and work guidance.

Matrix structures: designs for an organization's structures that allow for great cross-functional work to be done via delegated levels of leadership.

Opex: operational expenditure. Provision of funds to protect current organizational value.

Opportunity: a condition or situation favorable to a portfolio, program of work, or project that enhances value. Contrasts with Threat.

Organizational project management: a term used to imply an organization-wide adoption of project management techniques. Can be confused with portfolio management.

Outcome: achieved as a result of activity undertaken to effect change. Usually derived from program of work or project outputs. Outcomes are verified by benefits management or value capture processes.

Output: the tangible deliverable(s) from activity performed under a planned program of work or project.

P3M: an acronym for portfolio, program, and project management.

P3M governance: the functions, accountabilities, responsibilities, processes, and procedures that define how portfolios, programs of work, and projects are approved, initiated, set up, managed, and controlled.

Phase gate: a P3M governance mechanism where decisions are made at identified points, which determine the continuation or otherwise of investment initiatives.

Portfolio: a collection of programs of work, projects, and other work grouped together to facilitate effective management of that work to meet strategic business objectives. The content of each portfolio may not necessarily be interdependent or directly related.

Portfolio management: the centralized management of one or more portfolios to achieve strategic objectives.

Portfolio management office: See EPMO. (Can also refer to program management office at a business unit level.)

Program: a group of related projects, subprograms, and program activities that are managed in a coordinated way to obtain benefits not available from managing them individually.

Program management: the application of knowledge, skills, tools, and techniques to a program to meet the program requirements and to obtain benefits and control not available from managing projects individually.

Program of work: an extended view of program that allows for the inclusion of operational expenditure in addition to capital expenditure that is specific to program.

Program of work management: similar to program management but includes those management activities associated with efficient operation expenditure.

Project: a temporary endeavor undertaken to create a unique product, service, or result.

Reserve: an amount of funds (budget) or time needed above an estimate to reduce the risk of overruns of program of work and project objectives to a level acceptable to the organization.

Responsibility: used to describe the person who has permission and is expected to deliver outputs associated with programs of work and projects. Responsibility can be delegated.

Return on investment (ROI): an expression, often monetary based, that provides values of returns for investments made. Usually used in business cases.

Risk: an uncertain event or condition that, if it occurs, may have a positive or negative effect on an organization's business objectives and planned work.

Risk category: a grouping of potential causes of risk. Examples could be technical, external, organizational, or environmental. A category may include subcategories, such as technical maturity, weather, or aggressive estimating.

Risk management plan: the document describing how risk management will be structured and performed. Can apply to portfolio, program of work, or project management.

Risk management planning: the process of deciding how to approach, plan, and execute risk management activities for a portfolio, program of work, or specific project activity, either separately or collectively.

Risk threshold: defined levels of acceptability or deference toward certain risk levels.

Sponsor: a senior manager or executive who is accountable for portfolio, program of work, and project investment success.

Stakeholder: an individual, group, or organization that may affect, be affected by, or perceive itself to be affected by a decision, activity, or outcome of an initiative.

Steering group/committee: a governance-oriented group, usually chaired by a sponsor, that performs a governance function to portfolios, programs of work, and projects.

Strategic alignment: a term used in portfolio and program of work management to refer to the "fit" that portfolio and program of work plans have to business objectives from strategic plans.

Strategic goals: somewhat aspirational views on mid- to long-term desired position. Subset of organizational strategy.

Strategic implementation management: a high-level management mechanism that breaks down a strategic plan into defined actionable subplans for implementation purposes. Refer also to value management framework.

Strategic plan: a high-level document that explains the organization's vision and mission, plus the high-level approach that will be adopted to achieve the mission and vision, including identified goals and specific objectives to be achieved during the period covered by the document. Often long term in its outlook.

Talent management: defined policy and mechanisms that consider, seek, recruit, develop, and retain human resources for the organization.

Threat: a condition or potential condition that will have a negative effect of P3M activity. Contrasts with Opportunity.

Threshold: a governance mechanism that sets organizational boundaries or parameters for portfolio and program of work and project activity. Commonly expressed as a monetary amount.

Transformational: a term used to indicate a significantly sized change initiative that is often organization-wide.

Triggers: also referred to as risk symptoms or warning signs. Indications that an event has occurred or is about to occur. Triggers may have positive or negative effects, but generally trigger change.

Value capture: confirmation through measurement that the expected return on investment has been achieved. Refer also to Benefits Realization.

Value delivery: overarching term for the execution and controlling phase of any investment. Utilizes program of work and project management.

Value engineering: optimizing cost, schedule, and other attributes of a chosen solution without sacrificing quality.

Value management framework: the overall process of optimizing business investment, its function, and its return. Utilizes and integrates value strategy, value planning, value engineering, value delivery, and value capture.

Value planning: the process of assisting portfolio development by enhancing the use of portfolio management.

Value strategy: overarching policy that assists the organization to transform strategic plan content into actionable implementation plans that optimize the use of resources and maximize the value return.

Bibliography and References

The following books and articles were reviewed, referred to, or are referenced within the content of this book.

Association for Project Management (APM). (2006). *APM body of knowledge* (5th edition). High Wycombe, Buckinghamshire, England: Author.

AXELOS. (2011a). *Management of portfolios.* Norwich, England: The Stationery Office.

AXELOS. (2011b). *Managing successful programmes.* Norwich, England: The Stationery Office.

BDO. (2016). *Global risk landscape 2016 report.* BDO/Raconteur. London, England.

Bradley, G. (2006). *Benefits realisation management.* Aldershot, London, England: Gower.

Bridges, W. (1991). *Managing transitions: Making the most of change.* Boston, MA, USA: Addison-Wesley.

Collins, J. (2001). *Good to great: Why some companies make the leap and others don't.* New York, NY, USA: HarperCollins.

Crawford, J. K. (2001). *The strategic project office—A guide to improving organizational performance.* Boca Raton, FL, USA: CRC Press.

Economist Intelligence Unit. (2013). *Why good strategies fail: Lessons from the c-suite.* London, England: The Economist Intelligence Unit.

Fraser, I. (2003). *Benefits realisation: Balancing outputs with outcomes.* White paper. Project Plus Ltd.

Fraser, I. (2010). *The balanced scorecard overview.* White paper. Project Plus Ltd.

Fraser, I. (2014). *The war for talent is on: Are you strategically prepared?* Proceedings from PMI PMO Symposium. Miami, FL, USA.

Goleman D. (2000, March–April). Leadership that gets results. *Harvard Business Review,* 1–11.

Harkins, P. (1999). *Powerful conversations: How high impact leaders communicate.* New York, NY, USA: McGraw Hill.

Kanter, R. M. (1999). The enduring skills of change leaders. Leader to Leader 13. *Harvard Business Review.* (Reprinted in *Ivey Business Journal,* May–June, 2000, pp. 1–6.)

Kotter, J. P. (1987, 2012). *The leadership factor.* New York, NY, USA: Free Press.

KPMG. (2005). *KPMG global IT project management survey: How committed are you?* Retrieved from www.kpmg.com.

Lencioni, P. (2002). *Five dysfunctions of a team: A leadership fable.* Hoboken, NJ, USA: Jossey-Bass Inc.

Maxwell, J. (1998, 2007). *The 21 irrefutable laws of leadership.* Nashville, TN, USA: Thomas Nelson.

Nelson, K., & Aaron, S. (2005). *The change management pocket guide.* Cincinnati, OH, USA: Change Guides LLC.

Peters, T., & Waterman, R. (1982). *In search of excellence: Changing the way the world does business.* New York, NY, USA: HarperCollins.

Project Management Institute. (2012). *Pulse of the profession®: In-depth report: Organizational agility.* Newtown Square, PA, USA: Author.

Project Management Institute. (2013a). *A guide to the project management body of knowledge (PMBOK® guide) –* Fifth edition. Newtown Square, PA, USA: Author.

Project Management Institute. (2013b). *The standard for portfolio management – Third edition.* Newtown Square, PA, USA: Author.

Project Management Institute. (2013c). *The standard for program management – Third edition.* Newtown Square, PA, USA: Author.

Project Management Institute. (2015a). *PMI® thought leadership series: Delivering on strategy: The power of project portfolio management.* Newtown Square, PA, USA: Author.

Project Management Institute. (2015b). *Pulse of the profession®: Capturing the value of project management.* Newtown Square, PA, USA: Author.

Samoa High Commission. (2009). *The switch.* Wellington, NZ: Author.

Sanborn, M. (2006). *You don't need a title to be a leader.* Colorado Springs, CO, USA: WaterBrook Press.

Simmons, A. (2006). *The story factor* (2nd ed.). New York, NY, USA: Perseus Book Group.

Tate, K. (2005). *Project leadership—A practical guide to communicate, influence and collaboration.* Cincinnati, OH, USA: Griffin Tate.

W.L. Gore & Associates. (2015). *Our culture.* Retrieved from www.gore.com.

Index

Reader Reviews

"Never before has value creation mattered so much and been so achievable—in its time, of its time, for our time, for all time."
—Sarah Ross, PhD, Visiting Professor,
SKEMA Business School

"To challenge your thinking and gain new insights on business value, read this stimulating book."
—Mark Sanborn, Author of *The Fred Factor*
and *You Don't Need a Title to Be a Leader*

"For busy, business savvy directors, senior business executives and consultants—an absolute must-read. An illuminating game changer for dynamically improving strategy development and implementation through values driven, business integrated portfolio management."
—Chris Till, MA, Chief Executive,
Human Resources Institute of New Zealand

"This book stands out by its brilliant and intelligent simplicity to bring the right message to high-level leadership. It should be on top of the reading list of C-level executives and senior managers."
—Louis J. Mercken, MBA, PMI Fellow, Past PMI Chair
and Senior Advisor to the Board of the Threon Group

"In business, the wins and losses are measured by the ability to execute strategy at pace. Boosting organizational value through portfolio management offers a pragmatic, proven, and practical framework for organizational alignment and change management. Well done, Iain!"

—Craig Bunyan, MBA,
GM Technology, ANZ Banking Group

"The depth of knowledge shared by Iain in this publication makes it an absolute must-have, go-to reference for business professionals of all levels. The articulation around portfolio management and its application to the value management framework, as well as the introduction to the 3 Ps to Success as a critical approach to businesses is outstanding. An absolute must-read."

—Rommy Musch, Past Global Chair,
PMO SIG Group